BEYOND THE BOX

Great tasting, budget friendly, easy-to-follow recipes

JEN BREWER & ASHLEY WANGEMANN

FRONT TABLE BOOKS | AN IMPRINT OF CEDAR FORT, INC. | SPRINGVILLE, UTAH

Special thanks to Elena and Ramsey Kiefer for photographing the front cover image and the following recipes: Party Slush Punch, Spinach Dip, Bruschetta, Mango Salsa, Orange Julius, Blender Whole Wheat Pancakes, Irish Oatmeal, Breakfast Casserole, Whole Wheat Buttermilk Waffles, Eggs Benedict, Low Fat Wheat Blueberry Muffins, Pumpkin Pancakes, Maple Syrup, Sweet & Sour Chicken, Cheesy Chicken and Broccoli, Chicken Curry, White Lasagna, Sweet & Sour Meatballs, Sloppy Joe, Shepherd's Pie, Black Bean Burger, Hummus, Taco Soup, Cheesy Broccoli & Potato Soup, Oatmeal Pumpkin Bread, Slow Cooker Fudge Cake, Chocolate Lasagna, and Mac & Cheese.

Special thanks to Tiffany K. Peterson for photographing the following recipes: Black Bean Salsa, Teriyaki Flank Steak, and Chilled Strawberry Soup.

Special thanks to Christina G. for photographing the following recipes: Olive Oil Pizza Dough, Homemade Spaghetti Sauce, Carrot Cupcakes, and Butternut Squash Tacos.

Special thanks to Charla and Emily Fenn for photographing the following recipes: White Chicken Chili, Cafe Rio Creamy Tomatillo Dressing, Quinoa Salad with Avocados, Tres Leches, Yogurt Popsicles, and Cilantro Lime Rice.

Special thanks to Judith Scharman Draughon for photographing Acadian Black Beans & Rice.

Special thanks to Andrew Edwards for photographing Chicken Tortilla Soup.

Special thanks to Megan Byrd for photographing Turkey Vegetable Soup.

ISBN 13: 978-1-4621-4096-1

Published by Front Table Books, an imprint of Cedar Fort, Inc.
2373 W. 700 S., Springville, UT 84663
Distributed by Cedar Fort, Inc., www.cedarfort.com

Library of Congress Control Number: 2021948800

Cover & interior page design by Shawnda T. Craig

Printed in the United States of America

10 9 8 7 6 5 4 3 2 1

Printed on acid-free paper

CONTENTS

Introduction 1
Time, Money, Sanity 2
Appetizers 10
- Fruit Dip 11
- Bean Dip 12
- Salsa Fresca 13
- Cinnamon & Brown Sugar Almonds 14
- Roasted Pumpkin Seeds 15
- Party Slush Punch 16
- Spinach Dip 19
- Bruschetta 20
- Mango Salsa 22

Breakfast 23
- Orange Julius 24
- Blender Whole Wheat Pancakes 27
- Irish Oatmeal 28
- Broccoli & Cheese Quiche with Potato Crust 31
- Breakfast Casserole 32
- Whole Wheat Buttermilk Waffles 35
- Eggs Benedict 36
- Low-Fat Whole Wheat Blueberry Muffins 39
- Pumpkin Pancakes 40
- Maple Syrup 42

Fish 43
- Salmon Zucchini Linguini 44
- Fish En Papillote 46
- South of the Border Fish Tacos 47

Chicken 48
- Thai Lettuce Wraps 49
- Arroz Con Pollo 50
- Crockpot Chicken & Dressing Bake 51
- Southwest Pulled Chicken 52
- Chicken Salad 53
- Chicken Tinga 54
- Chicken Alfredo 55
- Chicken Cordon Bleu 56
- Sweet & Sour Chicken 59
- Cheesy Chicken & Broccoli 60
- Chicken Curry 63
- Lemon Pesto Chicken 64
- Make It Easy Chicken 67
- 7-Up Chicken 68
- White Lasagna 71
- Basil Chicken Pasta 72
- Chicken Pizza with Pesto Sauce 74
- Penang Curry 75
- Angel Hair Pasta & Chicken 76

Beef 77
- Sweet & Sour Meatballs 78
- Sloppy Joes 81
- Shepherd's Pie 82
- Teriyaki Flank Steak 85
- Stew 86

Pork 87
- Basic Pork Chops 88
- Creamy Parmesan & Bacon Pasta 91
- BBQ Ribs 92
- Cafe Rio Pulled Pork 95

Beans 96
- Acadian Black Beans & Rice 97
- Cowboy Caviar 99
- Black Bean Burgers 100
- Black Bean Salsa 102
- Avocado Black Bean Salad 103
- Best Crockpot Chili 105
- White Chicken Chili 106
- Hummus 109
- Butternut Squash Tacos 110

CONTENTS

Soup 112
- Taco Soup 113
- Minestrone 114
- Chilled Strawberry Soup 117
- Cheesy Broccoli & Potato Soup 118
- Chicken Tortilla Soup 121
- Zuppa Toscana 122
- Turkey Vegetable Soup 125
- Tomato Soup 126

Salad/Dressing 128
- Cafe Rio Creamy Tomatillo Dressing 129
- Turkey, Black Bean & Orzo Salad 130
- Quinoa Salad with Avocados & Black Beans 133
- Strawberry Salad with Poppyseed Dressing 134
- Thai Chicken Salad 137
- Mexican Black Bean Salad 138

Bread 140
- Olive Oil Pizza Dough 141
- Artisan Breads 143
- Oatmeal Bread 144
- Oatmeal Pumpkin Bread 147
- Basic Bagels 149
- Cornbread 150
- Breadsticks 153
- Pretzels 154

Dessert 156
- Tres Leches 157
- Banana Oat Chewies 158
- Pumpkin Muffins 161
- Carrot Cupcakes 162
- Butterscotch Oatmeal Cookies 165
- Fruit Crisp 166
- Yogurt Popsicles 169
- Rice Pudding 170
- Slow Cooker Fudge Cake 173
- Strawberry Trifle 174
- Chocolate Lasagna 177
- Nice Cream 178

Sides 180
- Cilantro Lime Rice 181
- Potato Wedges 182
- Amazing Fried Rice 185
- Mac & Cheese 186

Make Your Own 188
- Better than the Packet Taco Seasoning 189
- Pesto 190
- Homemade Spaghetti Sauce 191
- Homemade Cocoa Mix 192
- Muffin Mix 195

Appendix 197

Non-Recipe Meals 198

Measuring Equivalents 201

Common Spices 201

Food Yields 203

Serving Sizes of Common Foods 204

Spice Combination for Ethnic Dishes 205

Preparation Ideas for Fruits 206

Preparation Ideas for Vegetables 207

Ripening of Fruits and Vegetables 208

"Planned" Overs 208

Leftover Cake 210

Food Substitutions 211

Storage Time for Fresh Food 212

Storage Time for Frozen Food 213

Beef Cuts 214

Glossary 215

Index 216

About the Authors 219
- Jen Brewer 219
- Ashley Wangemann 220

INTRODUCTION

In a society where home-cooked meals seem to be reserved for those with time, money, and great kitchen skills, grabbing a box and adding water may seem like the default meal plan.

We want to present a different option. By learning a few tips and tricks, along with some easy to follow, budget friendly recipes, you can eat great-tasting, well-rounded meals that keep the money in your wallet and the weight off your waistline.

More than just recipes, Beyond the Box is full of kitchen tips, efficient tool suggestions, and plenty of reference charts that give you at-a-glance aids to elevate your kitchen experience. Drawn from the knowledge of experienced cooks and dietitian professionals, this book has a wealth of information to get you started on your road to kitchen mastery.

The appendix covers topics from household converting measurements to ideas on turning leftovers into planned overs.

In a hurry? Skip to the section on non-recipe meals to get you fueled and on your way in a flash.

Not sure how to put it all together? Check out the sample seven-day menu, complete with shopping list.

The best thing about this book, however, is that while it's helping you reach beyond the box, it is also reaching beyond the borders. For the past several years we have been working with non-government organizations (NGOs) to help families who struggle with malnutrition. The money that you paid for this book will be used to help families all over the world eat beyond the box of poverty and gain access to nutrition lessons and family gardens.

DOUBLE MEANING. DOUBLE IMPACT.

Thank you for being part of the solution to help end world hunger.

—Jen Brewer, MA, RDN

—Ashley Wangemann

For more information go to careforlife.org

TIME, MONEY, SANITY

Three resources are constantly at play with one another when we look at meals and nourishment: time, money, and sanity. All three are important to consider in the running of a household, particularly in the kitchen. It is also important to note that in saving one, oftentimes you will be taking from another.

A dear mentor during college taught me this very important concept. Early in her marriage, as a stay-at-home mom with small children, she had more time than money. With that time, she did many things in the kitchen. She grew and canned many of her own vegetables. She made meals from scratch. As the kids grew and started leaving the house, she returned to work. Their money increased, but available time dropped dramatically. Instead of hours and days of canning each season, she would simply buy the canned or frozen food from the store.

Same result. Different allocation of resources.

So it will be with you. We have gathered plenty of tips and tricks in each of these three areas. The purpose is not to have you frantically incorporate every tip into your daily routine. Instead, view them as tools that can help you at different times and in different phases of your life.

• SAVE TIME •

MENU PLANNING

In preparation for this book, we reached far and wide for advice from both food experts and the moms and dads next door to find their best-kept secrets for general tips in the kitchen. By far, the most popular answer was "plan, plan, plan." Menu planning is one of the simplest yet most effective tools to save time, money, and sanity. The trifecta tip! Planning meals can be as elaborate or simple as you make it. Some people plan an entire month ahead. Others do it week by week. Though at first it may seem like you are spending more time in the planning phase, it will save time over the long run. Having a weekly or monthly plan already set will save you from having to make last-minute dashes to the store (or eating out) and save you time during the day in trying to figure out what you can make each night.

THE BEST WAY TO PLAN

- Shop your fridge (and freezer!) Find items that are on their way out or needing to be used up. List those foods that need to be eaten. Look for recipes that can utilize those foods in different ways. (For example, leftover taco meat can be up-cycled into burritos or baked into Shepherd's Pie (pg 82). Find the list of "planned overs" to help spur you on to more ideas (pg 208).
- Shop your pantry. Again, look for items that have been in there for a while and could be put to good use.
- Then check the grocery store specials. If they are having a great sale on chicken, include some chicken recipes in the menu. Sale items can be a great start in planning your menu.
- Write the menu, either taking a picture of the recipe, or noting where you found it.

- If you have kids at home, involve them in the planning. Studies show that kids who are actively involved in the planning and cooking of meals are much more likely to try new foods and eat what they cook.
- Having seven kids, this worked perfect for me. I got a picture frame collage with eight small frames. Each child picked one day and wrote what they wanted to make. Then they listed the ingredients in my notebook. I could check those with what I had on hand, and my shopping list magically formulated itself.
- Use the concept of theme days to help plan your menu: Rice Night, Taco Tuesday, Meatless Monday, Breakfast for Dinner, Soupy Saturday, and so on.
- Reduce the meat in your menus. Swapping beans for meat in soups and all dishes Mexican saves money and adds nutrients. When a recipe calls for meat, automatically cut it in half. For example, if you're making spaghetti with meat sauce, brown the entire pound of hamburger, but only use half in the sauce. Add a can of diced tomatoes or other veggies to the sauce and freeze the rest of the browned ground beef for another day (Trisha Brimhall, RDN, www.nutritiousintent.com).

WHAT IF YOUR TASTES CHANGE DURING THE WEEK?

- If you plan something on Wednesday that you don't feel like eating when Wednesday arrives, change it. It's not a marriage commitment. The beauty of planning is not that it forces you into a cut and dried eating pattern. The beauty is knowing that each week you have on hand what you need to make for seven dinners. Feel free to rearrange the meals throughout the week.

WHAT ABOUT THE LEFTOVERS?

- If you find yourself with more food on hand than you can eat in a given week, incorporate that into the plan.
- An inventive friend named leftover night Stake Your Claim night. She cleans out the fridge, and the first kids to arrive in the kitchen get first pick. Once I incorporated this day into the week, it was amazing how quickly the kids made it down for dinner on Stake Your Claim night.
- Still have leftovers that won't go away? Let them eat cake—of the leftover variety. Seriously! This recipe will help you get rid of this pesky no-one-wants-them-anymore leftovers. (Just don't tell them what went into the cake.) See pg 210 for the recipe.

OTHER TIME-SAVING TIPS

- Freezer and fridge inventory: Filling this out and keeping it on your fridge or freezer will save you time in scouring through the contents, as well as money that you don't have to spend buying something you already have buried in the catacombs of the deep freeze.
- Getting the store apps to your most frequented grocery stores can help you quickly search for deals.
- Drive-up shopping. Many grocery stores now offer online shopping with curbside pick-up. Not only will this save time you would have spent wandering the isles, but it also helps save money because you stay away from the stores' highly advertised impulse items.
- Pre-prep anything possible. Anytime you can make something ahead, do it. It will save both time and sanity. When you bring a bunch of produce home, instead of sticking it in

the soon-to-be-forgotten-until-it-stinks shelf, cut up and freeze things that will be used in baked or cooked items. Peppers and onions are perfect for this. Cutting up vegetables ahead of time will pay big dividends when it comes time to put everything together in the recipe. Utilizing the buying in bulk and storing (see appendix) will save both money and time, not to mention boost your nutrition. I am much more likely to toss peppers into a slow cooker of chili if I have some already chopped and frozen than to take the time to chop and add some in while I'm throwing everything else in.

- Make a mix. Making your own mixes are both healthier and time saving. Making muffins? Instead of hunting for each ingredient, using the muffin mix recipe (pg 195) can reduce the time to merely scooping out some of the mix. Great for mornings when time becomes a premium commodity.
- Only have one star at a time. If you are trying out a new main dish recipe, keep the sides simple. Even a sliced apple can serve as the fruit portion of dinner.
- Think outside the norm. Cereal dinners can count. On nights when life is crazy and menu plans have perhaps fallen through, resist the temptation for take-out. Instead, take in—check out your pantry. Cereal can be a great go-to dinner. Spend the time you do have on crazy nights sitting around the table together, not hunting for gourmet meals.

• SAVE MONEY •

SAVING WHILE SHOPPING

- Think outside the grocery store. Frozen fruit costs one-fourth the price at the dollar store compared to a grocery store. Certain food items are definitely money savers from a dollar store, but not all. And don't worry, the quality is just as good; just keep an eye on expiration dates (Trisha Brimhall, RDN, www.nutritiousintent.com).
- Pay attention to the cost per ounce (often found on the price label on the shelf). Many times something that seems less expensive will actually cost more because the package holds less food, even though the packaging may seem the same size (Lacy Ngo, MS, RD, www.mindfulnessinfaithandfood.com).
- Prep your own produce. Carrot sticks, celery sticks, and so on are much cheaper than pre-prepped produce. Plus, whole carrots taste so much better than baby carrots. Peel and use the stalk of the broccoli, cauliflower and so on (Trisha Brimhall, RDN, www.nutritiousintent.com).

DON'T SHOP TIRED, HUNGRY, OR IN A HURRY

- When you're tired, you won't care to compare or be able to focus on finding the most nutrition for your buck. Take a nap, then hit the store.
- If you're hungry, everything looks good. Research shows that you will spend up to 60 percent more, even on non-food items. You will fill up your cart with much more than you intended to buy. Grab a snack, then get your groceries.
- When you're in a hurry, you won't take the time to comparison shop. Stores count on this, and you can miss the better deal when not looking for the price per ounce breakdown. Often the lower priced smaller item costs more per ounce than buying a slightly bigger container.

LOOK HIGH AND LOW ON STORE SHELVES

- Food companies pay a premium for eye-level shelf space, and their prices usually reflect that. If you want a quick way to save, look either on the top or bottom shelves for the lower priced brands.
- Speaking of brands, another quick way to save is to look for off brands. Most store brands contain the same quality as name brands but come with a smaller price tag.

MAKE A LIST AND STICK TO IT

- Stores count on impulse buys and will put all sorts of "opportunities" along your shopping path. I have personally paid the price for not following my own rule on this. There have been times when I have run into the store for "that one thing" only to come out with a cart full of stuff and realize that I forgot to get "that one thing." Make a list and promise yourself that you will only shop the list while you are in the store.

SHOP FRESH FOOD

- A common misconception is that fresh food is more expensive. Dietitian Tamar Rothenberg points out a quick comparison: four ounces of a banana costs about 18 cents. The same amount of potato chips costs 27 cents. Fresh is often, though not always (I'm looking at you, avocado), best for your wallet and your waistline (www.tamarrothenbergrd.com).
- Shopping fresh food in season guarantees the lowest prices (and highest quality). Farmers markets are golden for getting great deals on great fresh food. Plus you know the food has been grown close by, reducing the carbon footprint required to bring it to your table. See this list for seasonal foods to see at a glance which fresh foods will be the cheapest in each season.

USE FROZEN PRODUCE

- Can't find fresh foods when you need it? Don't give frozen food the cold shoulder. Usually low cost, frozen produce offers the same nutrients as their fresh counterparts.
- Check for versatile blends to save prep time in the kitchen.

STOCK UP ON SHELF STABLES

From "cupboard to the table" is not a phrase you often use, but it is something you may start to incorporate. Canned foods can be nutritious and time saving. Common myths may give canned foods a bad rap, but there are many good reasons you can enjoy canned foods and other shelf-stable items.

They won't go bad. Canned foods are well sealed to prevent oxidation and keep them preserved for when you are ready to eat them. Tip: No preservatives or additives are required to keep them from going rancid.

They come in varieties to suit your needs. They can be found in reduced-sodium and low sodium varieties. So, if you are watching your sodium-intake, you have a choice. Did you know that rinsing and draining your canned foods can reduce sodium levels by up to 41 percent?

They are easy to stock and store. They come in typical sizes that stack and fit within a typical cupboard. From canned tuna to 15–ounce canned beans, you can pack a lot into your space, without much bulk.

They are a simple option. They are great for those days when you've run out of fresh beef, poultry or fish or when you want to supplement your meals and veggie dishes with even more plant-based goodness (Rebecca Clyde MS, RDN, CD https://nourishnutritionblog.com/).

From protein and Vitamin D packed tuna and canned salmon, to dried herbs and spices, canned food can be a part of anyone's economic and nutritious food plan.

BUY IN BULK

Buy extra produce or meat when it's on sale. Chop it all up and freeze the extra portions immediately.

Cheese can also be purchased in bulk. You can shred it yourself and freeze the extra (Rebecca Clyde MS, RDN, CD, https://nourishnutritionblog.com/).

I also like to just write "vegetable" on my shopping list and then see what's a good price at the store. Keeping your options open means you'll spend less than going to the store for a specific vegetable that might be more expensive (www.thedomesticdietitian.com; see also Brynn McDowell and (Rebecca Clyde MS, RDN, CD https://nourishnutritionblog.com/).

Larger dairy containers of yogurt are usually cheaper than individual packs and definitely go with canned beans and veggies (Bracha Kopstick RD beekaynutrition.com).

Cereal lasts a long time. When you see a cereal sale, stock up and store the extra.

Buy plain whole grains rather than pre-seasoned or kits, and choose cheaper ones such as barley or rice vs quinoa (Bracha Kopstick).

Find a store that offers items in bulk containers. Nuts, grains, and spices can be purchased in smaller quantities, especially if you are new to them and not sure if you will like them.

USE INGREDIENTS FOR MULTIPLE THINGS

When cooking chicken to shred, first boil it to cook. Then freeze the broth in ice cube trays and use it to flavor other dishes later.

If you know of a great sale on meat, find two or three recipes that use that meat in different ways. (Start with the most mildly seasoned dish; then you can use the leftovers in spicier dishes later.)

Side dishes can often be incorporated into different meals. For example, corn can be used as a main side dish and then put into a stir fry or used in Spanish rice later in the week.

UTILIZE THE FREEZER!

If the recipe only calls for half an onion, chop the whole thing and freeze the other half to save time the next time a recipe calls for onions. You can also do this with peppers.

Have extra apples during apple season? Prepare the "guts" to an apple pie (the filling part), place in a Ziploc freezer bag, put in a pie tin, and freeze until hardened. Then remove from the pie tin and store in the freezer for a quick apple pie in the middle of winter.

See the Planned Over page in the back of the book for more ideas on multi-tasking ingredients.

SAVE MONEY

CHANGE YOUR MIND(SET)

Instead of thinking, "I can't eat healthy on a budget," start looking for ways that you can eat healthy on a budget.

Involve others in your household and make it a game. How long can you make the food budget stretch? Who can come up with the most creative dinner ideas using only the ingredients found in the house? Saving money can be fun when everyone buys into the frame of mind.

Adding beans or lentils to dishes allows you to cut the meat in half but still provide a nourishing and satisfying meal. Beans and legumes are a fraction of the price of meat and poultry and boast protein, iron, and fiber (Jennifer Hunt, RDN, LD www.healthy-inspiration.com).

Skip the trip to your coffee shop or smoothie stand and spend the five dollars instead on some fresh or frozen vegetables that you may talk about being "so expensive." Or get yourself a carton of eggs, which is easily one of the least expensive protein sources out there—less than a buck a serving (Mary Purdy, MS, RDN,—www.marypurdy.co).

COUPONING

One of the main sources people list for saving money at the store is through couponing. No, you don't need to go to the extreme couponing level to make a dent in your food budget. Countless people spend hours upon hours each week meticulously combing through every coupon magazine, clipping in duplicate and triplicate. Scores of other people have incredible blogs and websites teaching others how to save big with coupons. Yes, this is one way to save money at the store. But realize that in saving big money, you are spending time. If you have the seconds (and sanity) to spare, go for it. This isn't a how-to-clip coupons book, as so many others have mastered the art much more skillfully than myself. I will simply list some resources that specialize in this area:

- Pennypinchenmom.com
- hip2save.com
- couponmom.com
- Freestufffinder.com
- thekrazycouponlady.com
- thepennyhoarder.com
- Couponcravings.com
- Moneysavingmom.com

Here are some resources to help beginners get started:

https://thriftynomads.com/couponing-for-beginners-guide/

https://thekrazycouponlady.com/tips/couponing/5–easy-ways-to-start-couponing-now

http://moneypantry.com/beginner-couponing-guide/

Saving with couponing can be a great strategy. But remember that is takes time to dedicate to it on a daily basis.

A quick tip on couponing sites: Don't feel like you have to follow all of the advice on all of these sites. Each of these sites comes with their own personality and focus. Take some time, look around, and see which one or two gel with your likes and personality, and then stick with those.

Don't buy something just because you have a coupon for it.

Don't buy something just because you have a coupon for it. (Yes, it deserves repeating.)

In the end, it doesn't matter how much you save on a random box of food if it's not what you like to eat. It will end up sitting in your pantry for the next eternity until you finally do a major clean out and realize that it's two years past its expiration date!

Coupons for food items aren't the only way to save on groceries. In fact, the majority of food coupons are for overly processed foods. Instead of buying the prepared foods, stockpile other items (cleaning supplies, laundry detergent, deodorant, toothpaste, and so on), which clears out more money for fresh and healthy food.

If you are not a couponer and have no desire to become one, do not despair. That is not the only way to save.

INVEST IN SOME KITCHEN TOOLS

Some kitchen appliances, small and big, can pay for themselves many times over, not only in money save but also in time and sanity.

Find a freezer, even more than the small one attached to your fridge. A stand-alone freezer can stretch food and money in great dividends. You don't have to pay an arm and a leg, either. Check out garage sales, craigslist, or any of your neighborhood online sales. Chances are you'll find one for a fraction of the price of a new one.

Slow cooker. As writing this section, dinner is happily cooking in the slow cooker. It took about ten minutes to throw everything in this morning and saved me well over an hour of last-minute prep.

Muffin tins. Yes, they are for more than just muffins. They make great individually frozen portions of many foods you wouldn't normally consider. Meat loaf, corn bread, and even apple pie can all be cooked in individual portions in a muffin tin. Not only does this decrease the cooking time, but you can freeze these small portions and save time in defrosting them later. Other foods that can be frozen in muffin tin portions include smoothie leftovers, pesto, leftover soups, and shredded meat. Think outside the muffin mix and save yourself some time!

Pressure cooker. If you don't want to have to wait for a slow cooker to simmer all day, it might be worth investing in a pressure cooker. There are hundreds of sizes and brands out there. If you don't want to pay full price, hit up the thrift store near you. Chances are someone got one of these with the best of intentions, only to find they didn't want to take the time to learn the tips and tricks to use it.

MAKE MEAL PREP A FRIENDLY AFFAIR

Grab a group of friends and enlist them in a meal swap. Everyone picks their favorite go-to freezer friendly meal, then makes six of the same recipe (or however many are in the group). For the time you spend making your easy go-to dinner, you can exchange and get six different dinners, without having to invest the extra time in learning to make a new recipe.

Grab some girls together and make a freezer meal assembly line. Plan out a week (or the number of days you would like) of freezer-friendly recipes. Everyone pitches in to share the cost of the ingredients and meets up to spend the day catching up while assembling go-to meals for the busy weeks ahead.

Do a menu swap with friends. Have everyone write out a week's worth of menus (bonus if you all include a shopping list). Then gather them and share with each other. For the time it took you to plan out one week, you suddenly have ten to twelve weeks' worth of menus at the ready.

Organize a potluck with friends instead of eating out. Get creative and pick a theme night.

• SAVE SANITY •

Let's face it. Food preparation can be stressful. Sometimes it can push us to the edge. When funds are low and cravings are high, it's hard to stay within health and finance goals. Or 5:30 rolls around and we realize we have no plan or dinner. Normally, that's when we reach for the box, the quick fix, something to save the pull-out-the-hair moment. We've gathered some great tips from resources far and wide to help keep your sanity as intact as your budget.

START MEAL PLANNING IF YOU DON'T ALREADY

Are you sick of this one yet? Yes, this one can save time, money, and sanity. Try it out. Keep it simple. Organize a potluck with friends instead of eating out. Try a new recipe night, international night, appetizer night, restaurant knockoff night, and so on.

Make your grocery list on your phone. Or take a picture of it before you leave. I am too embarrassed to actually tell you the number of times I have pulled up to the grocery store only to realize I left my list right where I made it—on my kitchen table.

Become a "planned over" queen. Especially if you have kids, tweaking one tiny thing on a boring old leftover can change the moans and groans from the kids into songs of praise. Sanity saved.

FOOD TIPS TO KEEP YOU FROM PULLING YOUR HAIR OUT

If you over salted the soup, don't throw it out! Cut up some raw potatoes and throw them in. The potatoes will soak up the extra salt. Discard the potatoes once they have cooked and absorbed the extra salt.

If you want to skim the extra fat off soups or stews, put them in the fridge overnight. Fat will gel at the top. You can scoop it up and throw it out.

No time to wait overnight? Put in some ice cubes—the ice will collect some of the added fat.

Leafy green vegetables and celery store longer if you keep them in paper bags in the fridge instead of the plastic ones from the store.

To remove the core from a head of lettuce, slam it against the counter. Then dig your thumb right to the side of the core. It will pop right out. (This is also a great way to release stress!)

Hard brown sugar? No problem. Place a piece of bread in the container with it. It will soften in just a few hours. No time to wait? Either grate the brown sugar into the recipe or stick it in the microwave for fifteen-second intervals until it loosens up.

White sugar gone hard? Stick in the fridge for a day. The lumps will fall right out.

To keep old maids out of popcorn, store the kernels in the freezer.

Need to speed up the ripening of hard fruits or vegetables? Place in a paper bag on the counter. Need it even faster? Stick a banana in with it.

Realize in the middle of a meal that you are out of a spice? See food substitutions (pg 211) to find a substitute before saying some not nice words, then jumping in the car to make an extra trip to the store.

It's a constant ebb and flow between these resources. Again, don't feel pressured to suddenly incorporate every tip. Find the ones that you can do. Let the others go. Little changes will pay big dividends in building habits that will lead you to a lifetime of healthy, home cooking patterns. Realize in the middle of a meal that you are out of a spice? Use the substitution chart in the back of the book to find a substitute before saying some not nice words, then jumping in the car to make an extra trip to the store.

It's a constant ebb and flow between these resources. Again, don't feel pressured to suddenly incorporate every tip. Find the ones that you can do. Let the others go. Little changes will pay big dividends in building habits that will lead you to a lifetime of healthy, home cooking patterns.

APPETIZERS

ap·pe·tiz·er *(noun)*

a small dish of food or a drink taken before a meal or the main course of a meal to stimulate one's appetite.

FRUIT DIP

Serving size: ¼ cup • Serves: 14

NUTRITIONAL INFORMATION

Calories: 120 kcals • Carbohydrates: 21 g • Protein: 3 g • Fat: 2 g

MAKE AHEAD   QUICK AND EASY   VEGETARIAN/VEGAN   GREAT FOR A PARTY

INGREDIENTS

- 8 oz. fat-free cream cheese, softened
- 1 small jar marshmallow fluff (or ½ jar marshmallow topping)
- 1 small tub Cool Whip
- 1 cup strawberry yogurt

INSTRUCTIONS

1. Wash hands.
2. Whip cream cheese until light and fluffy.
3. Add marshmallow fluff (or topping) and Cool Whip. Mix until well blended.
4. Add yogurt and mix until smooth.
5. Refrigerate until ready to serve.

Variation: Try different flavors of yogurt.

Variation: Try Greek yogurt for added protein.

Tip: Use the leftover yogurt for a breakfast yogurt parfait (see non-recipe meals) or as an easy side for breakfast to add protein and calcium.

BEAN DIP

Serving size: ¼ cup • Serves: 14

NUTRITIONAL INFORMATION

Calories: 78 kcals • Carbohydrates: 7 g • Protein: 3 g • Fat: 3 g

MAKE AHEAD QUICK AND EASY VEGETARIAN/VEGAN HIGH FIBER GREAT FOR A PARTY

INGREDIENTS

1 cup refried beans

¾–1 cup salsa (If you prefer smooth bean dip, blend the salsa before adding it.)

4 oz. fat-free cream cheese

½ cup fat-free sour cream

½ cup shredded cheddar cheese

INSTRUCTIONS

1. Wash hands.
2. Place all ingredients (including cheddar cheese if using) in a microwave-safe bowl. Stir, but don't worry about getting it to combine all the way. It will come together as you heat and stir in the next steps.
3. Heat in the microwave on high for 1 minute and stir.
4. Continue heating in increments of 30 seconds, stirring after each time, until completely combined. Serve warm with tortilla strips.

Storage tip: Store in an air-tight container in the fridge for up to 1 week.

Variation: Use canned whole beans, any flavor, in place of the refried beans. Blend in a blender with salsa until smooth.

Variation: Use homemade salsa (pg 13) for a lower sodium version.

Use the leftover sour cream to make Arroz con Pollo (pg 50) or Chilled Strawberry Soup (pg 117)

SALSA FRESCA

Serving size: ½ cup • Serves: 6

NUTRITIONAL INFORMATION

Calories: 17 kcals • Carbohydrates: 3 g • Protein: 0.5 g • Fat: 0.5 g

MAKE AHEAD QUICK AND EASY VEGETARIAN/VEGAN

INGREDIENTS

2 medium tomatoes (quartered or chopped)

½ medium onion, chopped

cilantro or parsley (about 4 sprigs), chopped

2 garlic cloves, minced or chopped fine

1 tsp. garlic salt

2 Tbsp. lemon juice

jalapeño, chopped (seeds discarded; amount of jalapeño depending on desired heat: ⅓ for mild, ⅔ for medium, all for hot and spicy)

INSTRUCTIONS

1. Wash hands.
2. Mix all ingredients together.
3. Blend ingredients together for a smoother texture (optional).
4. Serve with chips, taco salad, tacos, burritos, and so on.

Storage tip: Store in an air-tight container in the fridge for up to 1 week.

Nutrition tip: This salsa is a great substitute for the high sodium salsa you can buy at the store.

This would be a great topping for South of the Border Fish Tacos (pg 47) or as a side with Cilantro Lime Rice (pg 181)

Use this salsa as part of the Bean Dip (pg 12), Cafe Rio Pulled Pork (pg 95), or Acadian Black Beans and Rice salad (pg 97)

Recipe courtesy of Julia Squires

CINNAMON & BROWN SUGAR ALMONDS

Serving size: 2 Tbsp • Serves: 6

NUTRITIONAL INFORMATION

Calories: 128 kcals • Carbohydrates: 10 g • Protein: 4 g • Fat: 9 g

MAKE AHEAD   VEGETARIAN/VEGAN   HIGH FIBER   GREAT FOR A PARTY   PREP TIME REQUIRED

INGREDIENTS

1 egg white

½ tsp. vanilla

4 oz. raw almonds (about ¾ cups)

2 Tbsp. brown sugar

1 Tbsp. sugar

¼ tsp. salt

½ tsp. cinnamon

INSTRUCTIONS

1. Wash hands.
2. Preheat oven to 250 degrees.
3. In a small bowl, whip egg white and vanilla until very frothy.
4. Stir in the almonds until well coated.
5. In a separate medium-sized bowl, combine sugars, salt, and cinnamon. Pour egg-coated almonds in the cinnamon sugar mixture and mix well.
6. Line a large baking sheet with parchment paper (or coat with non-stick spray) and spread almonds in an even layer on the sheet. Bake, stirring every 15 minutes until dry (about 45–50 minutes).
7. Store in an airtight container.

Tip: This makes a great healthier holiday snack or Christmas gift.

Use extra almonds to make a fresh Strawberry Salad (pg 134) or Banana Oat Chewies (pg 158)

ROASTED PUMPKIN SEEDS

Serving size: ¼ cup • Serves: 4

NUTRITIONAL INFORMATION

Calories: 92 kcals • Carbohydrates: 9 g • Protein: 3 g • Fat: 5 g

MAKE AHEAD VEGETARIAN/VEGAN BUDGET SAVER

INGREDIENTS

1 cup pumpkin seeds, clean and dry

2 tsp. olive oil

½ tsp. salt

⅛ tsp. paprika (optional)

⅛ tsp. chili powder (optional)

INSTRUCTIONS

1. Wash hands.
2. Wash pumpkin seeds in warm water to get off all the gooey pumpkin insides.
3. Spread seeds onto a clean surface and allow to dry completely.
4. Preheat oven to 350 degrees.
5. Once dry, combine the seeds, oil, salt, paprika, and chili powder in a bowl. Stir to coat. Spread the seeds in a single layer on a parchment paper-lined baking sheet.
6. Bake for 20 minutes, stirring them once after 10 minutes for more even cooking.
7. Let cool completely, and store in an air-tight container. Best when eaten within 5-7 days.

Tip: This is a great way to use up the pumpkin seeds after carving the jack-o-lanterns at Halloween time.

Tip: Pumpkin seeds are full of fiber and protein, making this a power-packed snack.

PARTY SLUSH PUNCH

Serving size: 1 cup • Serves: 6

NUTRITIONAL INFORMATION

Calories: 191 kcals • Carbohydrates: 49 g • Protein: 0 g • Fat: 0 g

MAKE AHEAD GREAT FOR A PARTY PREP TIME REQUIRED

INGREDIENTS

1 cup water

1½ cups sugar

1 quart cran-raspberry juice

1 quart unsweetened pineapple juice

1 liter Sprite or 7-up

INSTRUCTIONS

1. Wash hands.
2. Add water and sugar to a medium saucepan. Bring to a boil and stir frequently until sugar dissolves completely. Remove from heat and allow to cool slightly (about 10 minutes).
3. Combine cran-raspberry juice, pineapple juice, and sugar mixture in a container.
4. Freeze until slushy, about 3 hours. While this is freezing, place Sprite (or 7-up) in the fridge.
5. Pour Sprite into a large punch bowl. Add slushy juice mixture. Do not stir. To serve, ladle into cups. Or, fill cups ¾ full with Sprite and add a few spoonfuls of the slushy mixture to each cup.

Serving tip: This is a great drink to take to a party or gathering or for a special occasion.

Substitution tip: You can use Diet Sprite or Diet 7-up to lower the calories.

Tip: Use the left over 7-up for 7-up Chicken (pg 68).

Recipe courtesy of Ann Eldredge

SPINACH DIP

Serving size: ¼ cup • Serves: 8

NUTRITIONAL INFORMATION

Calories: 97 kcals • Carbohydrates: 8 g • Protein: 13 g • Fat: 5 g

MAKE AHEAD | QUICK AND EASY | VEGETARIAN/VEGAN | GREAT FOR A PARTY

INGREDIENTS

1 (1-oz.) packet original ranch party dip (or original ranch dressing mix)

2 cups (1 pint) low-fat sour cream

1 (10-oz.) pkg. frozen spinach, thawed, drained, and chopped

1 (8-oz.) can water chestnuts, chopped

INSTRUCTIONS

1. Wash hands.
2. Mix ranch dip and sour cream in a medium bowl.
3. Add spinach and water chestnuts. Stir.
4. Serve with chips, crackers, or veggies.

Tip: The spinach in this recipe gives a great boost to your bones and blood with the vitamin K and iron it contains.

Variation: Stir in slivered almonds to increase the protein.

Recipe courtesy of Ann Eldredge

BRUSCHETTA

Serving size: 1½ Tbsp. (on top of 1 slice of baguette) • Serves: 18–20

NUTRITIONAL INFORMATION

Calories: 94 kcals • Carbohydrates: 7 g • Protein: 3 g • Fat: 6 g

QUICK AND EASY VEGETARIAN/VEGAN SERVES A CROWD

INGREDIENTS

1 pint (2 cups) cherry tomatoes, sliced into small pieces

10-oz. bag (about 1 cup) mozzarella cheese balls

2 tsp. olive oil

1 tsp. salt (or more to taste)

½ tsp. balsamic vinegar (or more to taste)

4–5 leaves of basil, chopped into fine pieces

1 loaf baguette bread

butter, softened

INSTRUCTIONS

1. Wash hands.
2. Heat oven to broil.
3. In a medium bowl, mix together cherry tomatoes, cheese, olive oil, and salt.
4. Add balsamic vinegar and basil leaves. Stir just until blended. Set aside while preparing the bread.
5. Slice and butter baguette bread.
6. Place bread in a single layer on a cookie sheet and broil for 1–2 minutes, until slightly golden. This will happen fast! Don't step away from the oven. It can go from golden to burnt in seconds.
7. Spoon 1 Tbsp. bruschetta mixture onto each slice of bread.
8. Serve immediately.

Serving tip: If not able to serve immediately, keep bruschetta mixture in a bowl and place bread on a plate. Let the guests put it together during the meal.

Variation: Omit the bread and serve with croutons for a bruschetta salad.

Variation: Use balsamic glaze instead of balsamic vinegar.

Variation: This recipe is very forgiving. The amounts of each ingredient can be changed depending on taste.

MANGO SALSA

Serving size: ¼ cup • Serves: 4

NUTRITIONAL INFORMATION

Calories: 14 kcals • Carbohydrates: 1 g • Protein: 0 g • Fat: 0 g

MAKE AHEAD · VEGETARIAN/VEGAN · QUICK AND EASY · VARIATION ON TRADITIONAL RECIPE

INGREDIENTS

1 large mango, chopped

½ small jalapeño, diced and seeded (optional)

1–2 Tbsp. cilantro leaves, diced

¼ small red onion, diced

juice of ½ lime (1 Tbsp.)

salt to taste (about ¼ tsp.)

INSTRUCTIONS

1. Wash hands.
2. Stir mangos, jalapeño, cilantro leaves, and red onion together in a medium bowl.
3. Cut the lime into quarter sections and squeeze the juice over the salsa.
4. Add salt to taste, if desired.
5. Serve with chicken, fish, black beans and rice, or chips.

Mangos give a good dose of vitamin C, helping to boost your immune system.

Variation tip: For a smoother texture, blend ingredients together in a blender.

Storage tip: Store in an air-tight container in the fridge for up to 1 week.

Use this salsa as part of the Avocado Black Bean salad (pg 103).

BREAKFAST

break·fast *(noun)*

a meal eaten in the morning, the first of the day.

ORANGE JULIUS

Serving size: ¾ cup • Serves: 6

NUTRITIONAL INFORMATION
Calories: 120 kcals • Carbohydrates: 27 g • Protein: 2 g • Fat: 0 g

VEGETARIAN/VEGAN QUICK AND EASY

INGREDIENTS

1 (6-oz.) can frozen orange juice concentrate

1 cup milk

1 cup water

¼ cup sugar

1 tsp. vanilla

6 large ice cubes

INSTRUCTIONS

1. Wash hands.
2. Pour all ingredients into the blender and blend until smooth.
3. Pour and enjoy immediately.

Buy a large container of frozen orange juice concentrate and use the leftovers to make Yogurt Popsicles (pg 169) for a refreshing and healthy treat.

BLENDER WHOLE WHEAT PANCAKES

Serving size: 1 4–inch pancake • Serves: 8

NUTRITIONAL INFORMATION (per 2 pancakes)
Calories: 46 kcals • Carbohydrates: 4 g • Protein: 2 g • Fat: 3 g

VEGETARIAN/VEGAN HIGH FIBER FREEZES WELL MAKE ONCE EAT TWICE

INGREDIENTS

- 1 cup wheat kernels (yes, the kernels; they can be found in any whole foods store)
- 1½ cups milk, divided
- 1 egg
- 1 Tbsp. sugar
- 1 tsp. salt
- 1 Tbsp. baking powder
- ½ cup oil (or applesauce)

INSTRUCTIONS

1. Wash hands.
2. Put whole wheat into the blender.
3. Add 1 cup milk and blend at high speed for at least 3 minutes.
4. Add remaining milk and blend until smooth.
5. Add each of the remaining ingredients.
6. Blend until smooth, about 1-2 more minutes.
7. Cook on a hot griddle.
8. Serve with syrup, fresh fruit, whipped cream, peanut butter, or any other desired toppings.

Tip: The whole wheat kernels in this recipe are jam packed with fiber. These pancakes provide a hearty fill-you-up breakfast without overloading on calories.

Tip: Whole wheat kernels can be found in most bulk food areas, or in whole food grocery stores. They can be stored for years without going bad.

Substitution tip: Can use powdered milk if you don't have fresh on hand.

Substitution tip: Use skim milk for lower calories and fat.

Variation tip: Cut oil in half, or substitute applesauce in place of oil.

Variation tip: Add a banana while blending ingredients for a boost in potassium.

Recipe courtesy of Eileen Petersen

IRISH OATMEAL

Serving size: ¾ cup • Serves: 4

NUTRITIONAL INFORMATION (before additional toppings)
Calories: 80 kcals • Carbohydrates: 15 g • Protein: 2 g • Fat: 2 g

SLOW COOKER · VEGETARIAN/VEGAN · HIGH FIBER · MAKE ONCE EAT TWICE

INGREDIENTS

½ cup steel cut oats (Must be steel cut oats. Regular oats get very soggy.)

1½ cups fresh or frozen blueberries

½ cup of blueberry juice

1½ cups water

INSTRUCTIONS

1. Wash hands.
2. For best results: combine all ingredients in a slow cooker and cook for 2-4 hours on high or 4-6 hours on low until it reaches the consistency you like. Stir every hour or so. You can also cook longer without stirring as often, but you have to add more water and it come out a bit mushier. Add an extra ½-1 cup of liquid for 7-8 hours in the slow cooker.

Serving tip: Delicious when topped with a drizzle of organic maple syrup, honey, or a sprinkle of brown sugar.

Variation: if you don't have time to wait for the slow cooker, you can cook it over the stove top. Pour everything into a pan and bring to a boil. Reduce heat and simmer 45–50 minutes (until desired consistency), stirring occasionally.

Use leftover blueberries (fresh or frozen) to make Low-Fat Whole Wheat Blueberry Muffins (pg 39).

Serving tips: This quiche can be served hot or cold. It can be made the day before, covered with foil, and reheated in a 300-degree oven for 15 minutes.

Substitution tip: Add more veggies (tomatoes, bell peppers) for added fiber, vitamins, and minerals.

Substitution tip: If you are not a fan of broccoli, use a well-drained package of frozen,chopped spinach in its place.

Buy a large bag of frozen shredded potatoes and use the rest to make Breakfast Casserole (pg 32).

Use leftover broccoli to make Cheesy Broccoli and Potato soup (pg 60) or Amazing Fried Rice (pg 185).

BROCCOLI & CHEESE QUICHE WITH POTATO CRUST

Serving size: 1 slice • Serves: 8

Yields: one 10–inch pie plate

NUTRITIONAL INFORMATION

Calories: 222 kcals • Carbohydrates: 16 g • Protein: 13 g • Fat: 12 g

VEGETARIAN/VEGAN HIGH PROTEIN MAKE AHEAD

CRUST INGREDIENTS

3 cups shredded potatoes (may be frozen)

1 tsp. salt

¼ cup shredded Parmesan cheese

½ tsp. salt

½ tsp. ground pepper

1 Tbsp. melted butter

FILLING INGREDIENTS

1 Tbsp. butter

½ small onion, diced

2 cloves of garlic, minced

2 cups broccoli florets, diced

½ large red bell pepper, diced

5 large eggs

1 cup milk

1½ cups shredded cheddar cheese

½ tsp. salt

¼ tsp. ground pepper

INSTRUCTIONS FOR CRUST

1. Wash hands.
2. Preheat oven to 425 degrees and grease a 10-inch pie plate. Set aside.
3. Sprinkle salt over shredded potatoes and let sit for 10 minutes. Squeeze potatoes in a clean towel to remove all of the liquid (if using frozen hash browns, defrost, and squeeze all the water out).
4. In a large bowl, stir together dried potatoes, Parmesan cheese, salt, pepper, and melted butter.
5. Press mixture into the bottom and up the sides of the greased pie plate, making the layer of potatoes even.
6. Bake for 20 minutes, or until potatoes begin to brown. Remove from oven and let sit for 5 minutes before adding the filling.
7. Turn oven temperature down to 350 degrees.

INSTRUCTIONS FOR FILLING

8. In a large frying pan over medium heat, sauté onion, garlic, broccoli, and bell pepper in butter until onion is transparent and broccoli is bright green, about 5-8 minutes. Remove from heat.
9. In a large mixing bowl, whisk together eggs, milk, cheese, salt, and pepper
10. Spread broccoli mixture over potato crust in an even layer.
11. Pour egg mixture over broccoli mixture and evenly distribute everything throughout the quiche.
12. Bake in a 350-degree oven for 30 minutes, or until golden brown on top and egg mixture is set. Allow to sit for 10 minutes before cutting.

BREAKFAST CASSEROLE

Serving size: ½ cup • Serves: 9

NUTRITIONAL INFORMATION

Calories: 124 kcals • Carbohydrates: 5 g • Protein: 9 g • Fat: 7 g

MAKE AHEAD | VEGETARIAN/VEGAN | HIGH PROTEIN | HIGH FIBER | MAKE ONCE EAT TWICE

INGREDIENTS

13–14 oz. frozen shredded potatoes

2 tsp. seasoned salt, optional

1 tsp. salt

½–1 tsp. pepper

8 eggs

1¼ cup skim milk

1 cup cheese (cheddar, Colby jack, Monterey jack, etc. depending on flavor desired)

different kinds of veggies (zucchini, tomatoes, bell peppers, spinach, broccoli) or meat (optional)

INSTRUCTIONS

1. Wash hands.
2. Preheat oven to 350 degrees.
3. Grease a 9x13 pan. Pour the shredded potatoes into the pan and season with seasoned salt, salt, and pepper.
4. In a medium bowl, whisk together the eggs and milk. Stir in the cheese and any other desired filling.
5. Pour egg mixture over potatoes.
6. Cover with aluminum foil and refrigerate for 90 minutes. If low on time, put pan directly into the oven.
7. Bake for 90 minutes, covered with aluminum foil. Let sit for 10–15 minutes after removing from the oven.

Storage tip: A typical bag of frozen potatoes is 26 ounces. Use half for one batch and freeze the rest for another time.

Preparation tip: Whisk the eggs together first to ensure they are all mixed. Then Add the milk and other ingredients.

Tip: Cook once, eat twice.

Serving tip: This is a great recipe to make at the beginning of the week for a quick but warm breakfast the rest of the week.

Storage tip: Stays good in the fridge for 1 week, or freeze in single serving sizes to pull out later.

Use leftover frozen shredded potatoes to make Broccoli and Cheese Quiche (pg 31).

WHOLE WHEAT BUTTERMILK WAFFLES

Serving size: (1) 6 ½–inch waffle • Serves: 4

NUTRITIONAL INFORMATION (per 1 waffle)
Calories: 213 kcals • Carbohydrates: 24 g • Protein: 7 g • Fat: 9 g

MAKE AHEAD VEGETARIAN/VEGAN HIGH FIBER FREEZES WELL

INGREDIENTS

¾ cup buttermilk

2-3 Tbsp. butter or vegetable oil

1 egg, beaten

1½ tsp. vanilla

1 cup whole white wheat flour

1 Tbsp. sugar

1 tsp. baking powder

½ tsp. baking soda

INSTRUCTIONS

1. Wash hands.
2. In a large bowl, mix together buttermilk, melted butter (or oil), beaten eggs, and vanilla extract until thoroughly combined.
3. In a separate bowl, mix together flour, sugar, baking powder, and baking soda. Add to the wet ingredients and mix until just incorporated. Do not overmix.
4. Pour the desired amount of batter into the waffle maker and cook according to waffle maker directions.
5. Serve immediately.

Tip: The whole wheat in this gives a fiber boost to start your day.

Substitution tip: If you use oil instead of butter, add ¼ tsp. salt to enhance the flavor.

Variation tip: Cut oil in half, or substitute applesauce in place of oil/butter.

Store completely cooled leftovers in a Ziploc bag.

Freeze the leftovers for a fast breakfast later.

Use leftover buttermilk to make Cafe Rio Creamy Tomatillo Dressing (pg 129).

Recipe courtesy of Pennies and Pancakes

EGGS BENEDICT

Serving size: 1 sandwich • Serves: 4

NUTRITIONAL INFORMATION

Calories: 287 kcals • Carbohydrates: 27 g • Protein: 19 g • Fat: 11 g

HIGH PROTEIN

INGREDIENTS

4 English muffins

butter (enough to cover English muffins)

water to fill a large pot

1 tsp. oil

dash of salt

1 package hollandaise sauce (usually requires egg and milk to mix)

4 slices ham or Canadian bacon

4 eggs

INSTRUCTIONS

1. Wash hands.
2. Turn the oven to the broil setting.
3. Butter English muffins and place them on a cookie sheet. Place them in the oven and broil for about 2 minutes. Take out when lightly browned.
4. Heat water to a simmer. Add oil and a dash of salt.
5. Prepare hollandaise sauce according to package directions.
6. Place toasted English muffins around a plate. Put a piece of meat on each English muffin.
7. Crack egg and gently break to let the egg roll into simmering water. You can do several at one time, in different parts of the pot. Eggs should start to float within 2-3 minutes (signifying they are done). They will be white on the outside, with the yolk still slightly liquid on the inside. Gently scoop up with a slotted spoon to let extra water drain.
8. Softly place egg on top of meat. Repeat with remaining eggs. Scoop a small amount of hollandaise sauce over the top.

Substitution tip: For a vegetarian sandwich, use avocado slices, spinach, or tomato slices instead of meat.

Tip: Eggs provide a great source of protein to eat in the morning that will help you feel full longer.

Buy a large package of meat or get multiple slices from the deli and use leftovers to make Chicken Cordon Bleu (pg 56) or Amazing Fried Rice (pg 185).

LOW-FAT WHOLE WHEAT BLUEBERRY MUFFINS

Serving size: 1 medium muffin • Serves: 12

NUTRITIONAL INFORMATION

Calories: 163 kcals • Carbohydrates: 33 g • Protein: 7 g • Fat: 2 g

MAKE AHEAD · VEGETARIAN/VEGAN · HIGH FIBER · FREEZES WELL

INGREDIENTS

½ cup whole wheat flour (if no wheat flour on hand, can use white)

½ tsp. baking powder

¼ tsp. baking soda

¼ tsp. salt

1 egg

½ cup low-fat sour cream

3 Tbsp. bean puree

½ cup light brown sugar

½ cup rolled oats

½ cup blueberries (or ¾ cup frozen blueberries)

1 Tbsp. sugar

INSTRUCTIONS

1. Wash hands.
2. Preheat oven to 375 degrees.
3. Line muffin tins with paper liners. Spray liners to prevent muffins from sticking.
4. In a small bowl, combine flour, baking powder, baking soda, and salt; set aside.
5. In a large bowl, beat egg with sour cream until thoroughly combined. Add bean puree and brown sugar and mix just until combined. Stir in oats.
6. Fold flour mixture into the wet ingredients until just combined. Do not overmix.
7. Very gently fold in the berries.
8. Fill the muffin cups ⅔ full. Batter will be thick, so you may have to spread it out with the back of a spoon. Drop a generous pinch of sugar onto the top of each muffin.
9. Bake muffins for 25–28 minutes, or until the edges are medium brown and the tops are firm.
10. Cool for 5 minutes. Remove muffins (in their papers) and finish cooling them on a rack.

Variation tip: Add other types of berries (frozen or raw) in addition to blueberries.

Variation tip: Add a mashed banana to the wet ingredients for a boost in flavor and potassium.

Storage tip: Put extra muffins in a sealed bag to enjoy later. They stay good up to a week on the counter. Or freeze to save and eat later.

Use frozen blueberries to make Irish Oatmeal (pg 28) or use leftover sour cream to make Cafe Rio Creamy Tomatillo Dressing (pg 129) or Bean Dip (pg 12).

PUMPKIN PANCAKES

Serving size: (1) 4–inch pancake • Serves: 8

NUTRITIONAL INFORMATION (per pancake)
Calories: 80 kcals • Carbohydrates: 15 g • Protein: 2 g • Fat: 2 g

VEGETARIAN/VEGAN · MAKE ONCE EAT TWICE · FREEZES WELL · VARIATION ON TRADITIONAL RECIPE

INGREDIENTS

⅔ cup low-fat milk
6 oz. pumpkin puree
1 egg
2 tsp. vegetable oil
2 tsp. vinegar
1 tsp. vanilla
⅔ cup all-purpose flour
1 Tbsp. brown sugar
¾ tsp. baking powder
½ tsp. baking soda
½ tsp. ground allspice
½ tsp. ground cinnamon
¼ tsp. ground ginger
¼ tsp. salt

INSTRUCTIONS

1. Wash hands.
2. In a large bowl, mix together milk, pumpkin, egg, oil, vinegar, and vanilla.
3. In a separate bowl, combine flour, brown sugar, baking powder, baking soda, allspice, cinnamon, ginger, and salt. Stir into the pumpkin mixture just enough to combine; do not overmix.
4. Heat a lightly oiled griddle or frying pan over medium-high heat. Pour or scoop the batter onto the griddle, using approximately ¼ cup for each pancake.
5. Brown on both sides and serve hot.
6. Serve with fresh or frozen fruit, syrup, nut butter, and any other desired topping.

Nutrition tip: Pumpkin is a great source of vitamin A.
Tip: Freeze the leftovers.
Use leftover pumpkin to make Oatmeal Pumpkin Bread (pg 147) or Pumpkin Muffins (pg 161).

Recipe courtesy of Jolene Reed

BREAKFAST

MAPLE SYRUP

Serving size: 2 Tbsp. • Serves: 8

NUTRITIONAL INFORMATION

Calories: 113 kcals • Carbohydrates: 30 g • Protein: 0 g • Fat: 0 g

VEGETARIAN/VEGAN QUICK AND EASY

INGREDIENTS

½ cup water

1 tablespoon honey

½ tsp. maple extract

1 cup white sugar

2 Tbsp. brown sugar

INSTRUCTIONS

1. Wash hands.
2. Combine all ingredients in a small saucepan over medium heat on the stove.
3. Boil for 2 minutes.
4. Allow to cool for 5 minutes.
5. Carefully pour the syrup into prepared container.
6. Serve immediately.

Tip: A great way to save money is making your own syrup. Can be stored in an airtight container in the pantry.

Variation tip: If you like syrup a little on the thin side, try this variation: Boil 1 cup of water and add 2 cups of sugar. Stir just until dissolved. Heat until it returns to a boil. Take off heat and add 1½ tsp. maple flavoring.

FISH

fish *(noun)*

a cold-blooded animal that lives in water, breathes with gills, and usually has fins and scales. The meat of a fish is eaten as food.

FISH

SALMON ZUCCHINI LINGUINI

Serving size: ½ cup • Serves: 5–6

NUTRITIONAL INFORMATION

Calories: 153 kcals • Carbohydrates: 14 g • Protein: 11 g • Fat: 7 g

QUICK AND EASY BUDGET SAVER

INGREDIENTS

½ pound linguine

1½ tsp. olive oil, divided

2 Tbsp. walnuts, chopped

1 (8–9-in.) zucchini, sliced in ¼-in. discs

1 clove garlic, minced

¼ tsp. dried red pepper

7-oz. canned salmon, drained and skin removed

1 Tbsp. parsley, chopped

1½ tsp. fresh lemon juice

INSTRUCTIONS

1. Wash hands.
2. Bring a large pot filled with about 6 cups of water to a boil. Stir in pasta and cook according to package directions (approximately 9 minutes). Drain pasta in a colander, reserving ⅓ cup pasta water.
3. Meanwhile, heat 1 tsp. olive oil in a large skillet over medium heat. Add walnuts and cook for 5 minutes, stirring frequently. Remove walnuts from the pan and set aside in a small bowl.
4. Return pan to stove and add the remaining ½ tsp. olive oil. Add zucchini; cook 7 minutes, stirring occasionally until softened and lightly browned. Add garlic and dried red pepper. Cook for 1 minute.
5. Add salmon, drained pasta, and pasta water to zucchini. Stir gently to combine and heat through.
6. Garnish with chopped walnuts, parsley, and a squeeze of lemon juice.

Substitution tip: Can use fresh or frozen salmon instead of canned salmon.

Variation tip: Try with canned tuna if you already have it on hand.

Nutrition tip: Salmon is a great source of omega-3 fatty acids.

Use the other ½ lb. of linguine noodles to make Thai Chicken Salad (pg 137).

Recipe courtesy of Judy Barbe

FISH EN PAPILLOTE

Serving size: 1 fillet • Serves: 4

NUTRITIONAL INFORMATION

Calories: 212 kcals • Carbohydrates: 7 g • Protein: 31 g • Fat: 7 g

QUICK AND EASY

INGREDIENTS

4 large sheets parchment paper

4 pieces firm fish such as cod, halibut, or tilapia

2 cups mixed vegetables, chopped (zucchini, summer squash, onions, peppers, or frozen mixed vegetables)

4 tsp. butter

4 lemon slices

salt and pepper (to taste)

INSTRUCTIONS

1. Wash hands.
2. Preheat the oven to 375 degrees.
3. Lay a sheet of parchment paper on a cookie sheet.
4. Place one piece of fish on parchment. Top with ½ cup veggies, 1 tsp. butter, and a lemon slice. Shake some salt and pepper on top.
5. Fold the parchment paper on top of the fish and vegetables. Start at the corner near the fold. Turn and fold the parchment paper around the open edges to create a seal.
6. Repeat for the remaining 3 packets.
7. Bake for 12-15 minutes.
8. To serve, place packet on a plate and cut open carefully with a knife or kitchen shears.

Substitution tip: Use frozen or fresh fish.

Seasonal tip: Frozen mixed vegetables are a great option during the winter when there aren't as many vegetables in season—a great way to save money.

Buy a bag of frozen tilapia fillets and use the leftover fillets to make South of the Border Fish Tacos (pg 47).

Recipe courtesy of Dr. Pauline Williams www.williamsnutrition.net

SOUTH OF THE BORDER FISH TACOS

Serving size: 1 taco • Serves: 4

NUTRITIONAL INFORMATION

Calories: 60 kcals • Carbohydrates: 1 g • Protein: 11 g • Fat: 1 g

QUICK AND EASY

INGREDIENTS

2 white fish fillets (such as tilapia)

1 tsp. salt (to taste)

¼ tsp. pepper (to taste)

¼ tsp. paprika (to taste)

1 tsp. cumin (to taste)

1 tsp. chili powder (to taste)

½ tsp. garlic powder (to taste)

4 tortillas

possible toppings: cabbage (coleslaw), lime wedges, pico de gallo, sour cream, avocados

INSTRUCTIONS

1. Wash hands.
2. Cut fish into finger-sized pieces.
3. Season generously with salt, pepper, paprika, cumin, chili powder, and garlic powder.
4. Sear fish for about 3 minutes on the stove top or until browned.
5. Serve with tortillas, black bean salsa (pg 102), pico de gallo, sour cream, avocados, cabbage, or lime wedges.

Substitution tip: Use frozen or fresh fish.

Variation tip: Can use onion powder, oregano, or sriracha for additional flavor.

Buy a bag of frozen tilapia fillets and use leftover fillets to make Fish en Papillote (pg 46).

CHICKEN

chick·en *(noun)*

a domestic fowl kept for its eggs or meat.

THAI LETTUCE WRAPS

Serving size: ½ cup • Serves: 6

NUTRITIONAL INFORMATION

Calories: 101 kcals • Carbohydrates: 6 g • Protein: 7 g • Fat: 6 g

QUICK AND EASY

INGREDIENTS

½ head Iceberg lettuce

1 chicken breast, cooked and chopped to a very fine texture

2 Tbsp. Thai peanut sauce, divided

½ can water chestnuts, slivered

2 green onions, diced

⅓ cup peanuts, chopped

sweet chili sauce

INSTRUCTIONS

1. Wash hands.
2. Carefully separate lettuce leaves. Wash and then soak in ice water for 15-30 minutes and dry off.
3. Heat chicken with 1 Tbsp. Thai peanut sauce until warm. Add water chestnuts, onions, peanuts, and 1 more Tbsp. peanut sauce. Remove from heat.
4. Scoop mixture into lettuce leaf. Add peanut sauce and sweet chili sauce to taste.
5. Wrap and enjoy.

Preparation tip: Use a food processor to shred chicken.

Tip: Serve with rice for a great way to round out the meal.

Variation tip: Can be made without the peanuts.

Variation tip: Can serve on top of salad greens for a boost to any salad.

Use leftover peanuts to make Nice Cream (pg 178).

ARROZ CON POLLO

Serving size: ½ cup • Serves: 9

NUTRITIONAL INFORMATION

Calories: 210 kcals • Carbohydrates: 16 g • Protein: 16 g • Fat: 10 g

INGREDIENTS

4 Tbsp. butter

1 small onion, chopped

1 cup rice, cooked

1 clove garlic, chopped

2 cups water

1 cube chicken bouillon

3 Tbsp. frozen corn

2 cups chicken, cooked and shredded

1 can black beans, washed and drained

½ cup low-fat sour cream

1 cup green salsa

1 cup cheese

INSTRUCTIONS

1. Wash hands.
2. Preheat oven to 375.
3. In a pan, melt butter and fry onion for about 3 minutes.
4. Add rice and cook for another 2 minutes. Add garlic for a few seconds, and then add water and bouillon. Bring to a boil, reduce heat, and simmer for 10 minutes.
5. Add corn, cover, and cook for another 10 minutes.
6. Away from heat, mix together chicken, beans, sour cream, and green salsa.
7. Arrange half the mixture in a baking dish and add half the cheese.
8. Add the rest of the mixture, and finish with the other half of the cheese on top.
9. Bake for 10 minutes or until the cheese melts.
10. Garnish with fresh cilantro (optional).

Substitution tip: Use brown rice instead of white rice for added fiber.

Make a large batch of rice and use leftovers for Rice Pudding (pg 170), Amazing Fried Rice (pg 185), and Cilantro Lime Rice (pg 181).

CROCKPOT CHICKEN & DRESSING BAKE

Serving size: ½ cup • Serves: 8

NUTRITIONAL INFORMATION

Calories: 211 kcals • Carbohydrates: 23 g • Protein: 11 g • Fat: 6 g

SLOW COOKER

INGREDIENTS

1 box of Stove Top stuffing, made to instructions

2 chicken breasts, cooked and diced

1 cup frozen corn

1 can cream of chicken soup, mixed with ½ can milk

INSTRUCTIONS

1. Wash hands.
2. Preheat the oven to 350 degrees (or place mixture in a slow cooker on high).
3. Layer the stuffing in a 9 x 13 pan. Top with corn and chicken. Mix ingredients together.
4. Pour soup over the top.
5. Bake for 45 minutes in the oven (or 2 hours on high in a slow cooker).

Tip: A great way to use up extra vegetables from the fridge. Throw them in for a variation on flavor.

Recipe tip: Pour the milk into the can to help remove any leftover soup that is still in the can

Buy a bag of frozen corn and use the leftovers to make Arroz con Pollo (pg 50), Avocado Black Bean Salad (pg 103), or Mexican Black Bean Salad (pg 158).

CHICKEN

SOUTHWEST PULLED CHICKEN

Serving size: ½ cup • Serves: 4–5

NUTRITIONAL INFORMATION

Calories: 117 kcals • Carbohydrates: 6 g • Protein: 20 g • Fat: 2 g

SLOW COOKER FREEZES WELL

INGREDIENTS

2½ pounds boneless, skinless chicken thighs

1 small onion, chopped

1 clove garlic, chopped

1 small can tomato sauce

1 can chopped green chilis

3 Tbsp. cider vinegar

2 Tbsp. honey

1 Tbsp. sweet or smoked paprika

1 Tbsp. Worcestershire sauce

2 tsp. dry mustard

1 tsp. ground chipotle chile

½ tsp. salt

INSTRUCTIONS

1. Wash hands.
2. Stir all ingredients together in a 6-quart slow cooker. Put the lid on and cook for about 5 hours.
3. Transfer chicken to a cutting platter and shred with a fork. Return chicken to the sauce, stir well, and cook for another hour.
4. Serve on buns, over rice, with mashed potatoes, with roasted veggies, or any other desired dish.

Storage tip: Freezes well.

Variation: Experiment with different levels of spices. If you don't like one, you can cut it out, or substitute another one in.

CHICKEN SALAD

Serving size: ½ cup • Serves: 16

NUTRITIONAL INFORMATION

Calories: 216 kcals • Carbohydrates: 12 g • Protein: 23 g • Fat: 9 g

MAKE AHEAD · PREP TIME REQUIRED · GREAT FOR A PARTY · SERVES A CROWD · MAKE ONCE EAT TWICE

INGREDIENTS

2 boneless, skinless chicken breasts, cooked and cubed

¾ cup celery, chopped

½ cup red or purple grapes, sliced

¼ small onion, diced

2 Tbsp. dried cranberries

⅓ cup mayonnaise (more to taste)

salt and pepper (to taste)

INSTRUCTIONS

1. Wash hands.
2. Put cooked and cubed chicken in a large bowl. Mix in celery, grapes, onion, and dried cranberries. Stir in mayo. If not wet enough, add more mayo until satisfactory texture has been achieved. Add salt and pepper to taste.
3. If possible, refrigerate 24 hours before serving (it tastes better).

Substitution tip: Use the mayo with olive oil for reduced saturated fat.

Variation tip: Add cashews or almonds for an extra crunch and a boost of healthy fats.

Buy a whole package of celery and use the extras to make White Chicken Chili (pg 106), Minestrone (pg 114), or Turkey Vegetable Soup (pg 125).

Recipe courtesy of Treyce Stringer

CHICKEN TINGA

Serving size: ¾ cup • Serves: 8–10

NUTRITIONAL INFORMATION

Calories: 103 kcals • Carbohydrates: 4 g • Protein: 13 g • Fat: 4 g

MAKE ONCE EAT TWICE

INGREDIENTS

1 Tbsp. olive oil

1 large onion, sliced into rings

2-3 chipotle chilis (canned in adobo sauce)

3 tomatoes

1 garlic clove

1 cinnamon sticks

1 cube chicken bouillon

salt to taste (about ½ tsp)

1 pound chicken, cooked and shredded

1 Tbsp. brown sugar

INSTRUCTIONS

1. Wash hands.
2. Add oil to a pot and sauté onion on medium heat until softened (not browned).
3. In a blender, combine chipotle chilis, tomatoes, and garlic; puree until smooth.
4. Add puree to the onions in the pot. Add cinnamon stick, chicken bouillon, and salt. Bring to a boil. Reduce to a simmer for 10-15 minutes.
5. Add shredded meat and cook until heated, about 5 more minutes.
6. May serve with tostadas. Garnish with avocado and cheese or any other desired toppings.

Preparation tip: Shred chicken in a stand mixer (with paddle attachment).

Freeze the leftovers in single serving sizes to warm up for a quick lunch or dinner.

Serving tip: Pair with black beans, rice, and corn for a complete meal.

CHICKEN ALFREDO

Serving size: ½ cup • Serves: 4–5

NUTRITIONAL INFORMATION (for 5 servings)
Calories: 502 kcals • Carbohydrates: 43 g • Protein: 30 g • Fat: 24 g

CHICKEN

INGREDIENTS

½ pound angel hair pasta (or fettuccine)

⅓ cup butter

15-oz. container ricotta cheese

1 cup fat-free half and half

½ tsp. salt

½ cup grated Parmesan cheese

½ pound boneless, skinless chicken breast halves, cooked and cubed (cook with olive oil, Italian seasoning, and garlic powder if desired)

½ tsp. Italian seasoning

INSTRUCTIONS

1. Wash hands.
2. Cook fettuccine (or angel hair) pasta according to package directions.
3. In a large saucepan, melt butter. Add ricotta cheese, half and half, and salt. Stir until smooth and heated.
4. Add Parmesan cheese and stir until melted.
5. Stir in chicken and Italian seasoning.
6. Serve over cooked pasta.

Substitution tip: Use milk instead of half and half for fewer calories and less fat, or opt for a low-fat half and half.

Variation tip: Add vegetables (carrots, broccoli, bell peppers, spinach, tomatoes, artichokes, olives) for added fiber and micronutrients.

Use other ½ lb. angel hair pasta to make Angel Hair Pasta and Chicken (pg 76) and use leftover Parmesan cheese to make Basil Chicken Pasta (pg 72).

Pair with a breadstick (153), corn, and Caesar salad for a complete meal.

CHICKEN CORDON BLEU

Serving size: 1 piece • Serves: 4

NUTRITIONAL INFORMATION
Calories: 287 kcals • Carbohydrates: 20 g • Protein: 35 g • Fat: 8 g

PREP TIME REQUIRED

INGREDIENTS

2 chicken breasts, skinned, boned, and halved

½ cup shredded cheese

½ cup ham, finely chopped

2 tsp. mustard

1 egg

2 Tbsp. water

¼ cup flour

¼ tsp. salt

⅔ cup bread crumbs

oil for frying

INSTRUCTIONS

1. Wash hands.
2. Heat oven to 350 degrees.
3. Place chicken pieces between 2 pieces of plastic wrap. Working from the center out, lightly pound the chicken flat with rolling pin. (It's much easier if the store has thinly sliced chicken breasts on sale; then you can skip this step.)
4. In a small bowl, combine cheese and ham. Sprinkle chicken breasts lightly with salt; spread with mustard. Place ¼ cup cheese mixture on the center of each breast. Bring 1 end of breast over the cheese mixture. Fold in sides; roll up jelly roll fashion, pressing ends to seal. Cover; refrigerate at least 1 hour (if low on time, skip this step).
5. In a medium bowl, combine egg and water. In a shallow pan, combine flour and ¼ tsp. salt. Coat chicken with flour mixture; dip in egg mixture. Roll in breadcrumbs. Cover; refrigerate at least 1 hour (again, only if you have time).
6. In a small skillet, heat oil over medium heat. Fry each chicken roll about 2 minutes or until golden brown. Placed in a greased 2-qt. square baking dish or glass cake pan.
7. Bake for 25–30 minutes or until tender.

Purchasing tip: You can buy thinly sliced chicken breasts so you don't have to pound them down. Or have the butcher slice regular breasts to make them flatter.

Complete the meal by serving with mashed potatoes and low-sodium cream of chicken condensed soup as a sauce.

Use leftover ham to make Eggs Benedict (pg 36) or Amazing Fried Rice (pg 185).

SWEET & SOUR CHICKEN

Serving size: ¾ cup • Serves: 4

NUTRITIONAL INFORMATION

Calories: 164 kcals • Carbohydrates: 26 g • Protein: 13 g • Fat: 2 g

QUICK AND EASY

INGREDIENTS

½ cup pineapple chunks (reserve ½ cup juice)

¼ cup brown sugar

1 Tbsp. vinegar

2 ½ tsp. soy sauce

2 ½ tsp. cornstarch

2 Tbsp. ketchup

1 chicken breast, cooked and diced

INSTRUCTIONS

1. Wash hands.
2. Combine ½ cup reserved pineapple juice, brown sugar, vinegar, soy sauce, cornstarch, and ketchup in a medium saucepan. Bring to a boil for 1 minute.
3. Add pineapple chunks and chicken. Stir until heated through.
4. Serve over rice.

Variation tip: Serve over brown rice for added fiber.

Great way to use left over chicken.

Use leftover pineapple juice to make Sweet and Sour Meatballs (pg 78).

CHEESY CHICKEN & BROCCOLI

Serving size: 1 cup • Serves: 4

NUTRITIONAL INFORMATION

Calories: 188 kcals • Carbohydrates: 19 g • Protein: 20 g • Fat: 4 g

QUICK AND EASY

INGREDIENTS

1 pound cut broccoli, cooked and drained

1 cup cubed, cooked chicken

1 can Healthy Request cheese and broccoli soup

½ cup skim milk

⅛ tsp. pepper

4 saltine crackers, coarsely crushed (or 1 cup bread crumbs)

2-3 Tbsp. grated Parmesan cheese

½ tsp. Paprika

INSTRUCTIONS

1. Wash hands.
2. Preheat oven to 450 degrees.
3. In a cake pan, arrange broccoli and chicken.
4. In a small bowl, mix soup, milk, and pepper. Pour over the chicken/broccoli mixture.
5. In a small bowl, combine crushed crackers (or bread crumbs), cheese, and paprika. Sprinkle over the top.
6. Bake for 20 minutes, until hot and bubbling.

Nutrition tip: Broccoli is full of fiber, antioxidants, and many vitamins and minerals—it gives a great boost to your overall health.

Substitution tip: Use frozen broccoli if you don't have fresh on hand.

Variation: You can add some shredded cheese for a little kick.

Use leftover Parmesan cheese from Broccoli and Cheese Quiche (pg 31) or Basil Chicken Pasta (pg 72).

CHICKEN CURRY

Serving size: 1 cup • Serves: 4

NUTRITIONAL INFORMATION

Calories: 191 kcals • Carbohydrates: 11 g • Protein: 19 g • Fat: 9 g

QUICK AND EASY

CHICKEN

INGREDIENTS

1 onion, diced

1-2 Tbsp. curry powder (depending on spice level desired)

2 Tbsp. olive oil (however much to sauté your onions)

1 cup tomato sauce

1 ½ tsp. salt

2 chicken breasts, cooked and shredded

¾ cup water

INSTRUCTIONS

1. Wash hands.
2. Cook onions and curry powder in olive oil over medium heat for 10 minutes.
3. Add tomato sauce, salt, and chicken.
4. Cook uncovered for about 15 minutes or until the sauce looks "dry".
5. Add hot water, cover pot, and cook over medium heat for 5 minutes.
6. Serve over rice.

Preparation tip: Chop a large number of onions and put the rest in the freezer OR use frozen onions.

Variation tip: Add chopped vegetables (carrots, broccoli/cauliflower, bell peppers, peas, tomatoes) for added fiber and vitamins. See spice guide at back of book for alternate flavors.

Recipe courtesy of Torrey Olsen

LEMON PESTO CHICKEN

Serving size: ½ cup • Serves: 6

NUTRITIONAL INFORMATION
Calories: 234 kcals • Carbohydrates: 11 g • Protein: 27 g • Fat: 11 g

INGREDIENTS

1-1 ½ pound boneless, skinless chicken breast

1½ Tbsp. cornstarch

juice from 1 large lemon (about 6 Tbsp.)

3 Tbsp. pesto (pg 190)

2 Tbsp. plus 1 tsp. olive oil, divided

1 pound asparagus, washed, with woody ends removed

1 small onion, cut into ½ inch wedges

2 Tbsp. grated Parmesan cheese

¼ tsp. kosher salt

¼ tsp. fresh ground pepper

1 pint grape tomatoes

4-5 garlic cloves, peeled

INSTRUCTIONS

1. Wash hands.
2. Preheat oven to 425 degrees.
3. Cut chicken into uniform pieces, about 1½ inches, and place in a large bowl. Sprinkle cornstarch on top of chicken and mix until chicken pieces are evenly coated.
4. Add lemon juice, pesto, and 1 Tbsp. olive oil to chicken and stir to coat all pieces uniformly. Let sit while preparing asparagus.
5. Place prepared asparagus and onion in a one-gallon Ziploc bag or bowl. Add the remaining olive oil, Parmesan cheese, salt, and pepper. Close the zipper bag and mix ingredients by gently kneading and rubbing the bag (or mix in a bowl by hand).
6. Dump asparagus/onion mixture onto a large sheet pan. Spread out to the edges with space in the middle for the chicken. Pour chicken in the middle of the pan and spread out evenly.
7. Place grape tomatoes and garlic cloves on top. Bake for 25-30 minutes, or until chicken is heated to an internal temperature of 165 degrees.
8. Remove from oven and serve immediately. Goes nicely with whole grain pasta tossed with pesto.

Variation tip: For a crisper texture of cherry tomatoes, add them to the chicken and asparagus after they bake.

This is a great way to use up tomatoes and basil from the garden.

Use homemade pesto (pg 190) and leftover Parmesan cheese to make Breadsticks (pg 153).

Recipe courtesy of Marie, RDN https://healthyideasplace.com

MAKE IT EASY CHICKEN

Serving size: 1 cup • Serves: 4

NUTRITIONAL INFORMATION
Calories: 282 kcals • Carbohydrates: 14 g • Protein: 48 g • Fat: 5 g

SLOW COOKER MAKE ONCE EAT TWICE

INGREDIENTS

4 chicken breasts

salt and pepper (to taste)

3 carrots, peeled and chopped (more or less as desired)

1 medium potato, peeled and cubed (more or less as desired)

1 onion, diced (more or less as desired)

1 green bell pepper, chopped (more or less as desired)

½ tsp. thyme

½ tsp. basil

½ cup water

INSTRUCTIONS

1. Wash hands.
2. Sprinkle salt and pepper over chicken.
3. Place all ingredients in a slow cooker and cook on low for 6-8 hours.
4. Alternate: Cook at 350 degrees in an oven for 2 hours. If using frozen chicken, cook for 4 hours.

Storage tip: Make a batch of chicken and veggies at the beginning of the week and store in the refrigerator for up to a week for easy, simple meals

Peppers store great in the freezer. Buy a bunch, cut them up, and freeze to save time during recipe prep.

Use leftover carrots, potatoes, and bell peppers to make Stew (pg 86).

7-UP CHICKEN

Serving size: ½ cup • Serves: 8

NUTRITIONAL INFORMATION

Calories: 369 kcals • Carbohydrates: 8 g • Protein: 47 g • Fat: 19 g

PREP TIME REQUIRED GRILLS WELL

INGREDIENTS

1½ cups 7-Up

⅓ cup soy sauce

⅓ cup oil

½ tsp. horseradish

½ tsp. garlic powder

4–6 chicken breasts

INSTRUCTIONS

1. Wash hands.
2. Mix together all ingredients in a Ziploc bag and marinate for several hours in the refrigerator.
3. Grill chicken until no longer pink in the thickest part and until it reaches an internal temperature of 165 degrees.

Substitution tip: Use Diet Sprite to lower the calories.

Use leftover 7-Up to make Super Good Slush Punch (pg 16) for a party.

CHICKEN

WHITE LASAGNA

Serving size: ½ cup • Serves: 9 • Yields 1 9x13 pan

NUTRITIONAL INFORMATION

Calories: 526 kcals • Carbohydrates: 33 g • Protein: 32 g • Fat: 27 g

VARIATION ON TRADITIONAL RECIPE

INGREDIENTS

9 lasagna noodles

1 (15-oz.) container ricotta cheese

1 Tbsp. parsley

½ cup butter

½ cup flour

2 cups low-fat half and half

½ cup Parmesan cheese (optional)

1 pound chicken, cooked and cut into bite-sized pieces

2 cups mozzarella cheese

Italian seasoning (optional)

veggies of your choice–spinach, carrots, zucchini, artichokes (optional)

INSTRUCTIONS

1. Wash hands.
2. Prepare noodles according to package directions and set aside.
3. Mix ricotta cheese with parsley and set aside.
4. To make white sauce: melt butter in saucepan over medium heat. Stir in flour and salt, whisking constantly. While still stirring, pour in half and half and stir until thickened. Add Parmesan cheese (optional).
5. Preheat oven to 180 degrees.
6. To assemble, spray a 9x13 cake pan. Put a layer of noodles in the bottom. Pour some white sauce over the noodles and scoop ricotta cheese on top. Layer chicken mixture, and sprinkle mozzarella cheese on top. If desired, add vegetables before the mozzarella cheese. Repeat until you have as many layers as desired (2-3 layers).
7. Cover loosely with foil.
8. Bake for 25 minutes. Remove foil, bake for another 10 minutes until golden brown and bubbly.
9. Let stand 10 minutes then cut to serve.

Variation tip: Add veggies (spinach, carrots, zucchini, artichokes, olives, bell peppers, tomatoes) for added fiber and micronutrients.

BASIL CHICKEN PASTA

Serving size: ¾ cup • Serves: 4

NUTRITIONAL INFORMATION
Calories: 252 kcals • Carbohydrates: 34 g • Protein: 15 g • Fat: 7 g

INGREDIENTS

½ (12-oz.) box bow tie pasta
2 tsp. olive oil
1 chicken breast, cut in cubes
¼ tsp. garlic salt
½ cup milk
2 oz. cream cheese, cubed
¼ tsp. dried basil leaves
¼ cup grated Parmesan cheese

INSTRUCTIONS

1. Wash hands.
2. Cook pasta according to package directions.
3. Meanwhile, pour olive oil in a large skillet over medium heat. Add chicken and sprinkle with garlic salt. Cook until no longer pink.
4. Add milk and heat just until boiling. Stir in cream cheese and basil and reduce heat.
5. Stir constantly until cream cheese is completely melted and chicken is thoroughly cooked. Remove from heat.
6. Stir in Parmesan cheese. Toss pasta and sauce together and serve immediately.

Variation tip: Add extra veggies such as broccoli, carrots, bell peppers, spinach, and tomatoes.

Substitution tip: May substitute whole wheat pasta for a boost of fiber.

Use leftover Parmesan cheese to make Creamy Parmesan and Bacon Pasta (pg 91) or Breadsticks (pg 153).

CHICKEN PIZZA WITH PESTO SAUCE

Serving size: 1 slice • Serves: 8

NUTRITIONAL INFORMATION
Calories: 394 kcals • Carbohydrates: 14 g • Protein: 23 g • Fat: 26 g

BUDGET SAVER

VARIATION ON TRADITIONAL RECIPE

INGREDIENTS

1 pizza crust (homemade recipe on pg 141 or store bought)

1-2 cups pesto sauce (pg 190)

2 cup shredded mozzarella cheese or cheese blend

2 tomatoes, sliced

1 boneless, skinless chicken breast, cooked and chopped into bite-sized pieces

spinach, olives, artichokes, or other vegetables (optional)

INSTRUCTIONS

1. Wash hands.
2. Preheat oven to 425 degrees.
3. Spread pesto sauce on pizza crust.
4. Place cheese, tomatoes, chicken, and optional toppings on the pizza in desired order.
5. Place on cookie sheet and bake for 8-10 minutes.

Variation tip: Add other veggies to pizza such as olives, spinach, bell peppers, or .artichokes for extra fiber

A great way to use garden tomatoes and basil.

Use homemade pesto sauce (pg 190).

PENANG CURRY

Serving size: 1 cup • Serves: 4

NUTRITIONAL INFORMATION

Calories: 62 kcals • Carbohydrates: 5 g • Protein: 7 g • Fat: 2 g

INGREDIENTS

½ cup coconut milk

1 Tbsp. Penang curry paste

1½ tsp. chopped garlic

½ cup cooked chicken, cut into bite-sized pieces

1 Tbsp. fish sauce (optional)

1½ tsp. sugar

1 lime leaf

3 Thai basil leaves

INSTRUCTIONS

1. Wash hands.
2. Warm coconut milk in a wok or pan over medium heat, but don't let it boil.
3. Add curry paste and stir it until oil begins to separate and form a thin film, to bring out the maximum flavor.
4. Add the remaining ingredients except the lime and basil leaves.
5. Simmer until sauce is absorbed and thickened. Add lime and basil leaves. Stir fry briefly before serving.
6. Remove lime leaf and basil leaves before serving. Serve over rice.

Variation tip: Serve over brown rice for added fiber.

ANGEL HAIR PASTA & CHICKEN

Serving size: ½ cup • Serves: 4

NUTRITIONAL INFORMATION

Calories: 154 kcals • Carbohydrates: 11 g • Protein: 15 g • Fat: 6 g

INGREDIENTS

1 Tbsp. olive oil, divided

1 skinless, boneless chicken breast half, cut into cubes

½ lb. angel hair pasta

1 carrot, sliced diagonally (add as many as desired)

5 oz. frozen broccoli, thawed (add as much as desired)

1 clove garlic, minced

⅓ cup chicken broth

½ tsp. dried basil

2 Tbsp. grated Parmesan cheese

INSTRUCTIONS

1. Wash hands.
2. Heat 1 Tbsp. olive oil in a skillet over medium heat. Add chicken. Stir until chicken is done (about 5 minutes) and set aside.
3. Cook pasta according to pasta directions.
4. Heat remaining oil in the same skillet. Add carrot. Cook about 4 minutes. Add broccoli and garlic. Cook about 2 minutes longer, stirring,
5. Add chicken broth, basil, and parmesan to skillet. Stir to combine. Return chicken to skillet and simmer 4 minutes.
6. Drain pasta. Place in a large serving bowl. Top with chicken and vegetable mixture. Serve immediately.

Nutrition tip: The broccoli and carrots give vitamin A and antioxidants to keep your eyes healthy and boost your immune system.

Variation tip: Use more carrots for extra fiber and micronutrients.

Use the other half pound of angel hair pasta to make Chicken Alfredo (pg 55) and use leftover broccoli to make Amazing Fried Rice (pg 185).

BEEF

/bef/ (*noun*)

the flesh of a cow, bull, or ox, used as food.

SWEET & SOUR MEATBALLS

Serving size: 5 meatballs • Serves: 5

NUTRITIONAL INFORMATION

Calories: 316 kcals • Carbohydrates: 22 g • Protein: 16 g • Fat: 18 g

QUICK AND EASY

INGREDIENTS

½ large bag of meatballs (55-64 meatballs in package. Can use turkey meatballs)

1 red bell pepper, chopped

1 onion, chopped

4 oz. (½ can) pineapple tidbits: drain juice and save in another bowl

1 Tbsp. olive oil

¾ cup chicken stock

1 Tbsp. cornstarch

1 Tbsp. soy sauce

¼ cup reserved pineapple juice

2½ Tbsp. vinegar

¼ cup sugar

½ tsp. salt

INSTRUCTIONS

1. Wash hands.
2. Preheat oven to 350 degrees.
3. Put meatballs in a 9x13 baking dish.
4. In a separate pan, sauté bell peppers, onion, and pineapple tidbits in olive oil. Pour over meatballs.
5. In a medium saucepan, combine remaining ingredients and stir. Heat just to a boil while continuing to stir (mixture should thicken). Pour over meatballs.
6. Bake for 30 minutes in the oven, or until sauce bubbles.

Substitution tip: Use half a red and half a green bell pepper for a more colorful dish.

Prep ahead tip: If you have frozen onions and peppers, the chopping time to prep this recipe gets cut in half.

Use leftover meatballs for a meatball sub sandwich.

SLOPPY JOES

Serving size: ½ cup • Serves: 6

NUTRITIONAL INFORMATION
Calories: 362 kcals • Carbohydrates: 38 g • Protein: 20 g • Fat: 18 g

MAKE AHEAD   FREEZES WELL

INGREDIENTS

1 pound ground beef

½ large onion, chopped

1 garlic cloves, minced

4 oz. tomato sauce

1 (6-oz.) can tomato paste

¼ cup ketchup

2½ Tbsp. packed brown sugar

1½ Tbsp. soy sauce

6 hamburger buns, split and toasted

INSTRUCTIONS

1. Wash hands.
2. In a skillet, cook beef, onion, and garlic over medium heat until meat is no longer pink; drain any excess liquid or grease.
3. Stir in tomato sauce and paste, ketchup, brown sugar, and soy sauce. Mix well. Bring to a boil.
4. Reduce heat. Cover and simmer for 15-20 minutes, stirring occasionally.
5. Spoon about ½ cup meat mixture onto each bun.

Tip: Use 85 or 90 percent lean ground beef to save on fat and calories.

Prep tip: Cook the ground beef. Then rinse in cold water and pat dry with a paper towel to remove excess fat.

Variation tip: This recipe is easy to add veggies to without tasting them in the meal! Add carrots, bell peppers, or tomatoes for added fiber and vitamins/minerals.

Variation tip: For more of a kick, add some sriracha or a jalapeño pepper while cooking.

Storage tip: Make a double batch and freeze half of it in dinner for a quick meal.

Use leftover hamburger buns to make Black Bean Burgers (pg 100).

BEEF

SHEPHERD'S PIE

Serving size: ½ cup • Serves: 4–5

NUTRITIONAL INFORMATION
Calories: 351 kcals • Carbohydrates: 15 g • Protein: 21 g • Fat: 23 g

QUICK AND EASY

INGREDIENTS

1 pound ground hamburger, cooked and drained (and salted to taste)

1 can green beans, drained

1 can tomato soup (without diluting)

½-1 cup mashed potatoes (approximate)

¼-½ cup cheese

INSTRUCTIONS

1. Wash hands.
2. Preheat oven to 350 degrees.
3. Mix together hamburger, green beans, and tomato soup.
4. Cover with mashed potatoes.
5. Cover with cheese.
6. Bake for 20-30 minutes until heated through.

Variation tip: You can use this same idea with leftover roast and potatoes from Sunday dinner. Use the roast and any vegetables. Mix with gravy and top with mashed potatoes.

Use leftover cheese to make Breakfast Casserole (pg 32).

Recipe courtesy of Eileen Petersen

TERIYAKI FLANK STEAK

Serving size: ½ pound • Serves: 4

NUTRITIONAL INFORMATION

Calories: 389 kcals • Carbohydrates: 11 g • Protein: 48 g • Fat: 17 g

PREP TIME REQUIRED GRILLS WELL

INGREDIENTS

2 pounds flank steak

⅓ cup soy sauce

1½ tsp. seasoned salt

¼ cup chopped green onions with tops

1 clove minced garlic

1½ limes

2 Tbsp. brown sugar

INSTRUCTIONS

1. Wash hands.
2. Cut steak into 1-in. diagonal strips.
3. Combine all other ingredients and pour over steak strips.
4. Marinate overnight in the fridge.
5. Grill quickly, basting with marinade. Cook for about 4–7 minutes on each side, until desired degree of doneness (130–140 degrees for medium rare, 145 degrees for medium).
6. Let steak rest for 6–10 minutes to allow juices to disperse through steak.

Use other half of lime to make Mango Salsa (pg 22) or Mexican Black Bean Salad (pg 138).

STEW

Serving size: 1 cup • Serves: 8

NUTRITIONAL INFORMATION

Calories: 257 kcals • Carbohydrates: 19 g • Protein: 19 g • Fat: 11 g

SLOW COOKER

INGREDIENTS

½–1 pound of stew meat (or leftover beef of any kind)

3–4 carrots

2–4 potatoes

1 onion, chopped

1 (28-oz.) can stewed tomatoes

1½ tsp. beef bullion

½ cabbage head, chopped

3 cups boiling water

seasonings: salt, pepper, basil, oregano, thyme, bay leaves

INSTRUCTIONS

1. Wash hands.
2. Cook meat and carrots for 40 minutes on high in slow cooker (or on the stove).
3. Add potatoes, onion, tomatoes, bullion, cabbage, and water. Add extra seasonings as desired.
4. Cook for 2 hours on medium/medium high.

Variation tip: If cooking on the stove, simmer for 1 hour.

Prep tip: Save beef leftovers from other meals. Throw pieces into a freezer bag and let it fill up. When stew night comes, you'll already have the meat for it.

Use leftover vegetables to make Make It Easy Chicken (pg 67).

Recipe courtesy of Eileen Petersen

PORK

/pork/ (*noun*)

the flesh of a pig used as food, especially when uncured.

PORK

BASIC PORK CHOPS

Serving size: 1 chop • Serves: 4

NUTRITIONAL INFORMATION

Calories: 212 kcals • Carbohydrates: 1 g • Protein: 14 g • Fat: 14 g

10

PREP TIME REQUIRED

INGREDIENTS

4 loin chops (bone in or boneless)

1 tsp. salt

pepper to taste

½–1 tsp. garlic powder

1 tsp. onion powder

¼ tsp. cayenne pepper (if you want a little kick)

1 Tbsp. oil

INSTRUCTIONS

1. Remove pork chops from fridge and allow to rest on counter for 20 min. (This will help with cooking more evenly.)
2. Pat pork chops dry with paper towel.
3. Combine all seasoning ingredients in a small bowl and generously cover both sides of pork chops.
4. Heat oil in skillet on medium high heat.
5. Place pork chops in heated skillet and let cook 3–5 minutes, until a nice sear develops on the side (don't move pork chops around in pan).
6. Turn pork chops over, reduce heat to medium, and cover pan (the cover will help keep moisture in the pork chops).
7. Cook another 4–5 minutes, until internal temperature reaches 135 degrees.
8. Remove chops from pan and let rest for 5–8 minutes. They will continue cooking internally. Make sure temperature reaches 145 degrees before serving.

Variation tip: Substitute an Italian seasoning packet for the seasonings in the recipe for a nice twist on the basic pork chop.

Meat Choice: Boneless loins are generally easier to work with, but bone-in loins usually give more flavor and are a leaner cut of meat.

PORK

CREAMY PARMESAN & BACON PASTA

Serving size: ½ cup • Serves: 4–6

NUTRITIONAL INFORMATION

Calories: 289 kcals • Carbohydrates: 29 g • Protein: 14 g • Fat: 12 g

INGREDIENTS

½ pound lean bacon, cooked and crumbled

8 oz. ziti, penne, or similar pasta

¼ cup heavy cream

2 oz. reduced fat cream cheese

¼ cup grated Parmesan cheese, extra Parmesan to top

1 egg, beaten

⅛ tsp. black pepper

1 tsp. onion salt (optional)

INSTRUCTIONS

1. Wash hands.
2. Cook bacon as desired. Crumble and set aside.
3. While bacon is cooking, boil pasta in salted water according to package directions.
4. Place heavy cream and cream cheese in a small saucepan over low heat until cream cheese melts, whisking until smooth. Remove from heat and add Parmesan cheese, egg, and pepper. Whisk until blended.
5. Drain pasta (reserve a little of the liquid) and return to the pot. Immediately add sauce and toss to coat. The egg will be cooked by the hot pasta. Add some of the reserved pasta water if needed to loosen the sauce.
6. Stir in bacon, or sprinkle on top as desired. Add any desired vegetables. Serve hot immediately (sauce will lose its silkiness if standing too long).

Preparation tip: Microwaving the bacon with paper towels for 5–6 minutes will give you extra crispy bacon and soak up most of the grease.

Variation tip: Add vegetables for extra fiber and micronutrients (peas, sautéed onions or bell peppers, tomatoes, basil, spinach).

Use leftover bacon to make Zuppa Toscana soup (pg 122).

Recipe courtesy of Pennies and Pancakes

BBQ RIBS

Serving size: 2 ribs • Serves: 6

NUTRITIONAL INFORMATION

Calories: 266 kcals • Carbohydrates: 10 g • Protein: 14 g • Fat: 19 g

PREP TIME REQUIRED GRILLS WELL

INGREDIENTS

3-4 pounds spare ribs

½ tsp. salt

½ tsp. black pepper

2 small onions, sliced

2 Tbsp. apple cider vinegar

2 Tbsp. Worcestershire sauce

1 tsp. paprika

½ tsp. red pepper

1 tsp. chili powder

¾ cup ketchup

¾ cup water

INSTRUCTIONS

1. Wash hands.
2. Heat oven to 350 degrees.
3. Cut ribs into serving pieces. Season with salt and pepper.
4. Brown on a rack over a pan in the oven, or place ribs on the highest rack on a grill. Cover and cook at medium heat for 1 hour.
5. While ribs are cooking, combine all other ingredients. Stir and shake to make a sauce. Pour sauce over ribs.
6. Turn the oven down to 325 degrees, cover the ribs, and bake for 1½ hours. Uncover the last 15 minutes to brown more (until temperature reaches 145 degrees).
7. Sauce can also be used over chicken or beef.

Serving tip: Throw in some baked potatoes to cook alongside the ribs. Great for 4th of July or summer BBQs

Recipe courtesy of Barb Chase

CAFE RIO PULLED PORK

Serving size: ½ cup • Serves: 5–6

NUTRITIONAL INFORMATION

Calories: 332 kcals • Carbohydrates: 16 g • Protein: 40 g • Fat: 12 g

SLOW COOKER   FREEZES WELL

INGREDIENTS

1½ pounds pork roast

⅓ cup Worcestershire sauce

2 Tbsp. water

½ tsp. dried oregano

½ tsp. powdered ginger

½ tsp. salt

½ tsp. chili powder

½ tsp. garlic powder

1 tsp. dried minced onion

¼ cup brown sugar

5 oz. red enchilada sauce

INSTRUCTIONS

1. Wash hands.
2. Place pork roast in a slow cooker. Combine all ingredients except for brown sugar and enchilada sauce in a separate bowl.
3. Pour over roast and cook on low for 8 hours.
4. One hour before serving, take the roast out of the slow cooker and shred meat. Remove any fat. Drain the slow cooker and put the meat back in.
5. Add enchilada sauce and brown sugar. Stir together and cook for the last hour.
6. Serve with tortillas, black beans, and rice. Top with Salsa Fresca (pg 13), Black Bean Salsa (pg 102), or Cilantro Lime Rice (pg 181).

Serving tip: Use meat to make tacos, enchiladas, burritos, or salads.

Freeze leftovers for a great meal later.

This recipe goes well with Tomatillo Salsa (pg 13), Black Bean Salsa (pg 102), Cafe Rio Creamy Tomatillo Dressing (pg 189), and Cilantro Lime Rice (pg 181).

Recipe courtesy of Robin Hoelzle

BEANS

/ben/ *(noun)*

an edible seed, typically kidney-shaped, growing in long pods on certain leguminous plants.

(Acadian Black Beans & Rice on facing page)

BENEFITS OF BEANS

Not only are beans protein packed, they are also loaded with many more nutrients your body craves, including fiber, antioxidants, copper, folate, iron, magnesium, manganese, phosphorus, potassium, and zinc. That's a lot of bang for your buck—and bean! Beans almost always come out as one of the cheapest sources of jam-packed nutrition.

For more tips on cooking beans, recipes, and more, go to California Beans at tamarrothenbergrd.com/single-post/2017/09/13/Least-expensive-plant-foods

ACADIAN BLACK BEANS & RICE

Serving size: ½ cup • Serves: 6

NUTRITIONAL INFORMATION

Calories: 185 kcals • Carbohydrates: 32 g • Protein: 7 g • Fat: 4 g

MAKE AHEAD | QUICK AND EASY | VEGETARIAN/VEGAN | MAKE ONCE EAT TWICE

INGREDIENTS

1 Tbsp. olive oil

1 yellow onion, chopped extra fine

2 large bell peppers (any color), chopped

1 garlic clove, minced

1 can black beans, drained and rinsed

½ cup prepared salsa (can use homemade recipe on page 13)

1 bunch parsley, chopped (can use dried if needed)

1 bunch cilantro, chopped (can use dried if needed)

1 tsp. garlic powder

1 tsp. onion powder

1 tsp. thyme

1 tsp. oregano

½ tsp. cayenne pepper (leave out for a mild flavor)

¼ tsp. pepper

½ tsp. salt

1½ cups brown rice, cooked

INSTRUCTIONS

1. Wash hands.
2. If using already prepared brown rice, pull out from the fridge or freezer and set aside.
3. In a large skillet, heat oil to medium and add onion and bell peppers. Sauté until onions are transparent, about 5 minutes.
4. Add all other ingredients (except rice) to the large skillet with onion and bell pepper. Cook for 5 minutes.
5. Add the rice and heat through. Serve immediately.
6. Allow leftovers to cool to room temperature. Package in containers and freeze up to 6 months.
7. To prepare after freezing: Remove from the freezer and put in the refrigerator for at least 6 hours. It will keep in the fridge for 3 days. When serving, put in a large skillet and heat through. You can add more vegetable broth or salsa if it becomes too dry while heating. Alternate: microwave for 2-3 minutes until heated through, stirring every minute.

Serving tip: Tastes great warmed up or cold, which makes it great for batch cooking and taking to work for lunch.

Tip: If you have leftover cooked rice, this recipe will only take 10–15 minutes to cook.

Variation tip: Add avocado for a boost of healthy fats.

Variation tip: Add cherry tomatoes for a boost of fiber and vitamins.

Use homemade Tomatillo Salsa (pg 13) in this recipe and use leftover rice to make Rice Pudding (pg 170).

Recipe courtesy of Susan Watson www.alittlenutrition.com

COWBOY CAVIAR

Serving size: ½ cup • Serves: 16

NUTRITIONAL INFORMATION

Calories: 50 kcals • Carbohydrates: 10 g • Protein: 2 g • Fat: 0 g

MAKE AHEAD | QUICK AND EASY | VEGETARIAN/VEGAN | SERVES A CROWD | GREAT FOR A PARTY

INGREDIENTS

1 can black beans, drained

1 can pinto beans, drained

1 can black eyed peas, drained

1 can Green Giant Shoe Peg corn, drained (optional; can use regular corn)

½ cup red pimento, drained

2 Tbsp. chopped fresh jalapeño (or 1 can diced chili pepper)

8 green onions, sliced

1 yellow bell pepper, diced

1 orange bell pepper, diced

DRESSING INGREDIENTS

⅓ cup olive oil

¼ cup rice vinegar

¼ cup sugar

1½ tsp. salt

¼ tsp. pepper

INSTRUCTIONS

1. Wash hands.
2. Combine first 9 ingredients in a large bowl.
3. Cook the dressing ingredients until they boil; cool. Pour over bean mixture and mix together well.
4. Serve with chips or tortillas.

Serving tip: This recipe is a great dip to bring to parties or group gatherings.

Substitution tip: Use orange, red, or yellow bell pepper or a mixture of multiple colors for added color and vitamins and minerals.

Variation tip: Use more jalapeño for a spicier dip or omit it for a milder flavor.

This salad pairs well with BBQ Ribs (pg 92).

Recipe courtesy of Elena Schumacher

BLACK BEAN BURGERS

Serving size: 1 burger • Serves: 4

NUTRITIONAL INFORMATION

Calories: 260 kcals • Carbohydrates: 32 g • Protein: 11 g • Fat: 11 g

BUDGET SAVER

VARIATION ON TRADITIONAL RECIPE

INGREDIENTS

½ onion, chopped

2 Tbsp. olive oil

1½ cups cooked black beans, divided

1 garlic cloves, minced

2 eggs

¾ cup bread crumbs

½ tsp. liquid smoke

½ tsp. lemon pepper

¼ tsp. red pepper flakes

½ tsp. salt

4 hamburger buns

INSTRUCTIONS

1. Wash hands.
2. Sauté onions in 1 Tbsp. olive oil until they start to brown.
3. In a blender or with a potato masher, puree 1 cup beans.
4. Mix puréed mixture and remaining ½ cup beans with onions, garlic, eggs, bread crumbs, liquid smoke, lemon pepper, red pepper flakes, and salt.
5. Form into 4 patties.
6. Cook over griddle until they start to crisp on the outside and are warmed through.
7. Serve on hamburger buns with regular hamburger toppings.

Nutrition tip: A great way to pack in the protein without the added calories from regular hamburgers.

Variation tip: Add more or less liquid smoke depending on flavor desired.

Use leftover buns to make Sloppy Joes (pg 81).

BEANS

BLACK BEAN SALSA

Serving size: ¼ cup • Serves: 4

NUTRITIONAL INFORMATION

Calories: 70 kcals • Carbohydrates: 13 g • Protein: 4 g • Fat: 0.5 g

MAKE AHEAD VEGETARIAN/VEGAN QUICK AND EASY

INGREDIENTS

1 cup cooked black beans

½ cup corn, roasted and cooled (roasting optional)

1 red bell pepper, diced finely

½ bunch cilantro, chopped

2 green onions, sliced thin

½ red onion, sliced thin

1 Tbsp. lime juice

½ tsp. garlic, chopped

salt and pepper (to taste)

INSTRUCTIONS

1. Wash hands.
2. Combine all ingredients and mix well.
3. Taste for salt and pepper and adjust seasoning as needed.

Serve with tacos, salads, enchiladas,or eggs. A great boost to almost any meal.

Use leftover lime to make Mango Salsa (pg 22) or Cafe Rio Creamy Tomatillo Dressing (pg 129).

AVOCADO BLACK BEAN SALAD

Serving size: ¼ cup • Serves: 6–7

NUTRITIONAL INFORMATION

Calories: 195 kcals • Carbohydrates: 28 g • Protein: 6 g • Fat: 8 g

MAKE AHEAD VEGETARIAN/VEGAN QUICK AND EASY

INGREDIENTS

1 cans black beans, drained and rinsed

1¾ cup frozen roasted corn

1 cup mango, peach, or pineapple salsa (pg 22)

¼ cup fresh lime juice (2 limes)

2 avocados, diced

2 Tbsp. red onion, chopped fine

salt to taste

2 Tbsp. cilantro

jalapeños to taste, red pepper flakes, or hot sauce (optional)

INSTRUCTIONS

1. Wash hands.
2. Mix black beans, frozen corn, and fruit salsa together in a medium bowl.
3. Squeeze limes and set aside.
4. Add avocado to salad. Before mixing, immediately add lime juice, red onion, and salt to salad. Gently mix all ingredients together.
5. Add cilantro prior to serving.

Variation tip: To give the salad a little kick, add some hot pepper flakes, hot sauce, or a freshly diced jalapeño pepper.

Avocados are an excellent source of unsaturated fats.

Use leftover corn to make Black Bean Salsa (pg 102) or Arroz con Pollo (pg 50).

Recipe courtesy of Judith Scharman Draughon author of Lean Body Smart Life. www.foodswithjudes.com

BEST CROCKPOT CHILI

Serving size: 1 cup • Serves: 10

NUTRITIONAL INFORMATION
Calories: 126 kcals • Carbohydrates: 13 g • Protein: 8 g • Fat: 5 g

SLOW COOKER · HIGH PROTEIN · FREEZES WELL · MAKE ONCE EAT TWICE

INGREDIENTS

2 cans beans (black, kidney, chili, or anything you have on hand)

1 pound ground beef, cooked and drained

1 onion, diced

1 garlic clove, minced (or 1 Tbsp. minced garlic)

1 large green bell pepper, diced

1 cup diced carrots

1 (28-oz.) can crushed or stewed tomatoes

1 Tbsp. chili powder

1 Tbsp. cumin

1 tsp. black pepper

1 Tbsp. salt (to taste)

¼ tsp. cayenne pepper (can increase for added spice)

INSTRUCTIONS

1. Wash hands.
2. Pour everything into a slow cooker.
3. Cook on high for 2 hours, until mixture is combined and heated through. You can cook on low for several hours to keep warm and ready for dinner.
4. Serve with cheese, sour cream, chives, cilantro, avocado, or any other desired toppings.
5. Refrigerate leftovers or freeze in a Ziploc bag.

Variation tip: Add extra bell peppers and carrots for added fiber and vitamins.
Storage tip: Make a large batch and store in smaller containers for quick, reheat-able meals.
Serve with Cornbread (pg 150) for a great chili and cornbread combo!

WHITE CHICKEN CHILI

Serving size: 1 cup • Serves: 16

NUTRITIONAL INFORMATION

Calories: 101 kcals • Carbohydrates: 11 g • Protein: 11 g • Fat: 2 g

QUICK AND EASY · HIGH PROTEIN · VARIATION ON TRADITIONAL RECIPE · FREEZES WELL · MAKE ONCE EAT TWICE

INGREDIENTS

1 pound chicken breast, cubed

1 medium onion, chopped

2 carrots, cut into medium pieces (optional)

2 stalks celery, cut into small pieces (optional)

1 Tbsp. garlic powder (or 2 cloves minced garlic)

1 Tbsp. oil

2 cans Great Northern beans, drained

1 can chicken broth

1-2 small cans chopped green chilis (depending on spice level desired)

1 tsp. salt

1 tsp. cumin

1 tsp. oregano

1 tsp. pepper

½-1 tsp. cayenne pepper (depending on spice level desired)

½-1 cup low-fat sour cream

optional toppings: shredded Monterey Jack cheese, tortilla chips, lime juice

INSTRUCTIONS

1. Wash hands.
2. Sauté chicken, onion, garlic powder, and oil in a medium saucepan until chicken is cooked.
3. Add beans, broth, green chilis, carrots, celery, and spices. Bring to a boil, reduce heat, and simmer for 10 minutes.
4. Remove from heat. Add sour cream (and cheese if using it). Stir until melted and creamy.
5. Top with cheese, tortilla chips, lime juice, or any other desired toppings.

Variation tip: Add extra carrots and celery for a more colorful and vitamin-packed soup.

Storage tip: Make a batch and store leftover chili in smaller containers in the freezer for quick and easy meals.

Use leftover celery to make Chicken Salad (pg 53) or Minestrone (pg 114).

Recipe courtesy of Cheryl Darsow

HUMMUS

Serving size: 2 Tbsp. • Serves: 8

NUTRITIONAL INFORMATION

Calories: 156 kcals • Carbohydrates: 15 g • Protein: 4 g • Fat: 10 g

QUICK AND EASY VEGETARIAN/VEGAN HIGH PROTEIN BUDGET SAVER

INGREDIENTS

2-4 garlic cloves (depending on individual preference)

1 tsp. dried rosemary (may use leaves from fresh sprig if desired)

small pinch of red pepper flakes

1 can chickpeas (garbanzo beans), rinsed and drained

2 Tbsp. tahini paste

2 Tbsp. fresh lemon juice

¼-½ tsp. salt, as desired

olive oil, as desired

INSTRUCTIONS

1. Wash hands.
2. Grind garlic, rosemary, and red pepper flakes in a food processor.
3. Add chickpeas, tahini, and lemon juice and process more.
4. Add olive oil while continuing to process until creamy texture is reached.

Substitution tip: Use garlic powder instead of garlic cloves if you want an easier blend and less garlic flavor.

Serving tip: Eat hummus with some crunchy fresh veggies for a delicious and healthy snack.

Serving tip: Use hummus as a spread on sandwiches/wraps for added protein.

Use leftover lemon to make Lemon Pesto Chicken with Asparagus and Tomatoes (pg 64).

BUTTERNUT SQUASH TACOS

Serving size: ½ cup • Serves: 8

NUTRITIONAL INFORMATION

Calories: 187 kcals • Carbohydrates: 31 g • Protein: 8 g • Fat: 5 g

VEGETARIAN/VEGAN

VARIATION ON TRADITIONAL RECIPE

INGREDIENTS

1 can refried beans (or you can mash black beans)

1 Tbsp. olive oil

1 small butternut squash, peeled and cut into ½-in. cubes

1 tsp. salt

½ tsp. cinnamon

1 tsp. cumin

½ tsp. black pepper

corn tortillas

cilantro (to taste)

green salsa (to taste)

sour cream (to taste)

INSTRUCTIONS

1. Wash hands.
2. Warm beans in a small pan.
3. Heat a medium skillet over high heat and add oil. When it starts to smoke, add squash and toss well in the oil.
4. Sprinkle with salt, cinnamon, cumin, and pepper. Sauté over high heat, stirring frequently until squash is browned outside and tender inside (about 10 minutes).
5. To serve, heat tortillas in a hot, dry skillet. Assemble tacos by spooning in beans and topping with squash, cilantro, Black Bean Salsa (pg 102), and sour cream.

A great way to eat from the garden. Perfect twist on use for the overflow of squash.

Butternut squash is a great source of vitamin A and E.

Fun way to incorporate more plant based/meatless meals into your menu.

Use leftover green salsa to make Arroz con Pollo (pg 50).

SOUP

/soop/ (*noun*)

a liquid dish, typically made by boiling meat, fish, or vegetables, etc., in stock or water.

TACO SOUP

Serving size: 1 cup • Serves: 8

NUTRITIONAL INFORMATION

Calories: 359 kcals • Carbohydrates: 37 g • Protein: 19 g • Fat: 16 g

SLOW COOKER HIGH FIBER HIGH PROTEIN

INGREDIENTS

1 can of black beans, undrained

1 can of corn, undrained

1 (28-oz.) can diced tomatoes, undrained

1 can pinto beans, undrained

1 pound browned ground beef

1 package Hidden Valley Ranch dry dressing mix

1 package taco seasoning (or use homemade, recipe 98)

1-2 cups of water (enough to make it soup-like)

INSTRUCTIONS

1. Wash hands.
2. Add all ingredients to a slow cooker and let it cook on high for 2-4 hours. Or cook on the stove at low or medium heat for about an hour.
3. Serve with sour cream, cheese, lime, tortilla chips, or any other desired topping. Can also serve with quesadillas.

Nutrition tip: Packed with fiber and protein. This soup will fill you up before it fills you out!

Variation tip: Add some diced bell peppers or carrots for added fiber and vitamins.

Use homemade Taco Seasoning (pg 189) for this recipe.

MINESTRONE

Serving size: 1 cup • Serves: 8

NUTRITIONAL INFORMATION

Calories: 216 kcals • Carbohydrates: 42 g • Protein: 8 g • Fat: 3 g

VEGETARIAN/VEGAN HIGH FIBER

INGREDIENTS

1-2 Tbsp. olive oil

2 zucchini, cut into cubes

2-3 stalks celery, cut into small pieces

3 medium carrots, peeled and chopped

1 onion, finely chopped

other vegetables as desired (optional)

1 clove garlic

4 cups broth (vegetable, chicken, or beef)

1 (15-oz.) can kidney beans (or other desired type of bean—cannellini, white, Great Northern beans), drained and rinsed

1 (15-oz.) can crushed tomatoes

1 Tbsp. Italian seasoning

1 tsp. salt

1 tsp. pepper

½ pound pasta (small shell noodles, penne)

Parmesan cheese for topping (optional)

INSTRUCTIONS

1. Wash hands.
2. Heat a soup pot over medium-high heat and add the olive oil. Add the vegetables and garlic and stir until browned and beginning to soften, about 5-7 minutes.
3. Stir in the broth, beans, tomatoes, Italian seasoning, and salt and pepper. Bring the liquid to a boil.
4. Add pasta and simmer until pasta is al dente (or at your desired texture).
5. Serve immediately or turn to low to remain heating. May serve with Breadsticks (pg 153).

Minestrone helps you fill up on veggies and protein from the beans in a delicious way!

Tip: If you want a more filling/less liquidy soup, add an extra can of beans and extra carrots and celery.

Variation tip: Use whole wheat pasta for added fiber.

Use extra celery to make Chicken Salad (pg 53) or Turkey Vegetable Soup (pg 125).

CHILLED STRAWBERRY SOUP

Serving size: ½ cup • Serves: 8

NUTRITIONAL INFORMATION

Calories: 87 kcals • Carbohydrates: 6 g • Protein: 3g • Fat: 6 g

MAKE AHEAD | PREP TIME REQUIRED | MAKE ONCE EAT TWICE | VARIATION ON TRADITIONAL RECIPE

INGREDIENTS

1 cup fresh or frozen strawberries

1 cup milk

½ cup heavy cream

¼ cup sour cream

1 Tbsp. white sugar, or to taste

INSTRUCTIONS

1. Wash hands.
2. Puree strawberries, milk, cream, and sour cream in a blender or food processor until smooth. Stir in sugar to taste.
3. Chill 8 hours or overnight in the refrigerator before serving.

A great summer meal during strawberry season. A fun fruity take on soup!

Substitution tip: Use low-fat half and half and sour cream to save on fat and calories.

Use leftover sour cream to make Bean Dip (pg 12) or Low-Fat Whole Wheat Blueberry Muffins (pg 39).

Recipe courtesy of Ann Eldredge

CHEESY BROCCOLI & POTATO SOUP

Serving size: 1 cup • Serves: 6

NUTRITIONAL INFORMATION

Calories: 212 kcals • Carbohydrates: 17 g • Protein: 6 g • Fat: 14 g

VEGETARIAN/VEGAN MAKE ONCE EAT TWICE

INGREDIENTS

1¾ cups potatoes, peeled and cubed

¼ cup minced onion

¼ cup cubed carrots (optional)

½ head of broccoli cut up

1 quart water

3-4 chicken bouillon cubes

dash of minced garlic, parsley flakes, and salt and pepper

⅓ cup butter

½ cup flour

1 cup milk

½ cup cheddar cheese, grated

INSTRUCTIONS

1. Wash hands.
2. Combine potatoes, onion, carrots, broccoli, water, bouillon cubes, and seasonings in stock pot. Cover and simmer for 30 minutes or until potatoes are tender.
3. In a separate pan, melt butter. Add flour and whisk quickly. While whisking, slowly add milk. Once warmed and beginning to thicken, add cheese and stir until cheese is melted and mixture is smooth.
4. Pour into pot with potato mixture and stir to thoroughly mix.
5. Serve and enjoy.

Variation tip: Use whatever vegetables you have on hand and need to use up. You can also omit the cheese and turn it into a creamy soup.

Use other ½ head broccoli to make Amazing Fried Rice (pg 185).

CHICKEN TORTILLA SOUP

Serving size: 1 cup • Serves: 4–5

NUTRITIONAL INFORMATION (without toppings)
Calories: 174 kcals • Carbohydrates: 19 g • Protein: 17 g • Fat: 3 g

QUICK AND EASY HIGH PROTEIN

INGREDIENTS

2 tsp. olive oil

½ large onion, chopped

2 oz. diced green chilis

½ pound chicken, cooked and shredded

½ tsp. cumin

½ tsp. oregano

½ tsp. chili powder

½ tsp. garlic powder

7 oz. diced tomatoes

½ can small white beans

2 Tbsp. chopped fresh cilantro

1 cup chicken broth

¼ lime

salt and pepper (to taste)

avocado, cheese, sour cream (optional)

INSTRUCTIONS

1. Wash hands.
2. In a large pot, sauté onion and chilis with oil on medium heat. Sauté until tender.
3. Add chicken and spices and stir together.
4. Add tomatoes, beans, and fresh cilantro. Stir until combined.
5. Add broth and bring to a boil. Reduce heat and simmer 5 minutes or longer to bring out the flavors.
6. Add lime juice (or serve on the side) just before serving.
7. Ladle into bowls and garnish with avocado, sour cream, shredded cheese, tortilla strips, or any other desired topping.

Tip: A great way to use frozen chopped onions and use up other vegetables.

Storage tip: Freeze leftover green chilis and use for other recipe in the future.

Variation tip: For a little kick, Add ¼–½ tsp. cayenne pepper.

Nutrition tip: Add avocado for a boost of healthy fats.

Use leftover lime to make Mango Salsa (pg 22) or Teriyaki Flank Steak (pg 85).

Tip: Serve homemade tortilla strips with the soup (see glossary).

Recipe courtesy of: Anna Jensen

ZUPPA TOSCANA

Serving size: 1 cup • Serves: 4–5

NUTRITIONAL INFORMATION

Calories: 690 kcals • Carbohydrates: 25 g • Protein: 22 g • Fat: 57 g

Kale is one of the most nutrient dense foods, packed with vitamin C and K, as well as antioxidants and fiber.

INGREDIENTS

4 slices bacon, cut into small pieces

1 pound sausage with sage

½ tsp. red pepper flakes

½ large yellow onion, chopped very fine

4 cloves garlic, chopped fine or 2 tsp. minced garlic

4 cups chicken broth

3½ cups russet potatoes, cubed

salt and pepper (to taste)

¾ tsp. Mrs. Dash seasoning

2 cups loose packed kale, chopped in bite-sized pieces

1 cup heavy cream (or half and half or evaporated milk)

grated Parmesan cheese to top

INSTRUCTIONS

1. Wash hands.
2. In a large soup pot, cook bacon over medium heat until crispy. It is important to keep it over medium heat because you don't want the bacon to burn, just to get crispy.
3. Add sausage and red pepper flakes to bacon. Begin to break up the sausage to mix with the bacon. Cook until sausage is cooked all the way through on medium heat. Remove from heat and drain off the grease.
4. Add about 2 Tbsp. of the meat mixture into your soup pot and add chopped onion. Sauté onion until translucent. Add garlic and sauté until you really start to smell the garlic.
5. Add meat mixture back into the pot and add chicken broth and potatoes. Season with 1 ½ tsp. salt and ½ tsp. pepper and Mrs. Dash, or to taste.
6. Bring the mixture to a boil and turn heat to low to simmer until potatoes are tender (about 20 minutes).
7. Add kale and heavy cream. Bring back to a simmer and let it simmer until kale is wilted.
8. Sprinkle Parmesan cheese on top and serve.

Use leftover bacon to make Creamy Parmesan and Bacon Pasta (pg 91).

Variation: Use low-fat sausage and light half and half to save calories and fat.

TURKEY VEGETABLE SOUP

Serving size: 1 cup • Serves: 4

NUTRITIONAL INFORMATION
Calories: 187 kcals • Carbohydrates: 22 g • Protein: 14 g • Fat: 4 g

SLOW COOKER HIGH FIBER

INGREDIENTS

½ pound lean turkey
1 tsp. oregano
1 tsp. garlic powder
2 large carrots, chopped
2 stalks celery, chopped
½ onion, diced
1 large sweet potato, peeled and cubed
¾ cup green beans, chopped
2 Tbsp. fresh rosemary, minced
1 tsp. dried oregano
14-oz. can diced tomatoes
4 cups vegetable broth
salt and pepper to taste

INSTRUCTIONS

1. Wash hands.
2. Sauté turkey until brown. Season with oregano and garlic powder while it is cooking.
3. Add all ingredients to a slow cooker, as well as the sautéed turkey.
4. Slow cook on high for 6-8 hours. Serve and enjoy!

Tip: A great way to use leftover Thanksgiving turkey.
Tip: Use frozen green beans—they're just as healthy and require no pre-prep.
Tip: Sweet potatoes are a great source of vitamin A and fiber.
Use leftover celery to make White Chicken Chili (pg 106) or Minestrone (pg 114).

Recipe courtesy of Megan Byrd, RD www.theoregondietitian.com

TOMATO SOUP

Serving size: ¾ cup • Serves: 6

NUTRITIONAL INFORMATION
Calories: 104 kcals • Carbohydrates: 9 g • Protein: 2 g • Fat: 6 g

VEGETARIAN/VEGAN MAKE ONCE EAT TWICE

INGREDIENTS

2 Tbsp. butter

½ onion, chopped

1 tsp. chopped garlic (or 1 clove minced)

1 dried bay leaf (optional)

1 tsp. dried oregano

1 cup tomato juice

1 (28-oz.) can diced tomatoes, with juice

1 cup water

1 tsp. bouillon cube (or 1 tsp. Better Than Bouillon paste)

1 tsp. dried basil (or 3–4 fresh leaves, ripped into small pieces)

⅛ tsp. pepper (to taste)

⅛ tsp. salt (to taste)

½ cup half and half cream

INSTRUCTIONS

1. Wash hands.
2. Melt butter in large saucepan over medium heat. Add onions and garlic.
3. Sauté until onions are translucent.
4. Add everything except the half and half and bring to a boil. Cook about 10–15 minutes.
5. Spoon out the bay leaf (if using).
6. Pour into blender and blend until smooth.
7. Pour back into saucepan and add half and half.
8. Garnish with any of the following: cheese, sour cream, crackers, croutons, tortilla chip bits, or bacon bits.

GARDEN VARIATION: If you have a plethora of produce and want to use fresh tomatoes, use 2–2.5 pounds of roma tomatoes in place of the canned tomatoes and tomato juice. Slice tomatoes lengthwise and place on baking sheet. Drizzle with olive oil and salt. Bake at 375 degrees for 30–40 minutes, until slightly caramelized and softened. Pour tomatoes into sauce pan after step 3 and continue with the rest of the recipe.

SALAD/DRESSING

sal·ad *(noun)*

a cold dish of various mixtures of raw or cooked vegetables, usually seasoned with oil, vinegar, or other dressing and sometimes accompanied by meat, fish, or other ingredients.

CAFE RIO CREAMY TOMATILLO DRESSING

Serving size: 2 Tbsp. • Serves: 8

NUTRITIONAL INFORMATION

Calories: 43 kcals • Carbohydrates: 1 g • Protein: 0g • Fat: 4 g

MAKE AHEAD   PREP TIME REQUIRED

INGREDIENTS

1 fresh tomatillo, peeled and cut into quarters

juice from ¼ lime

2½ Tbsp. buttermilk

2½ Tbsp. mayonnaise

2½ Tbsp. low-fat sour cream

⅓ package ranch buttermilk dressing mix

⅓ cup fresh chopped cilantro

2 stalks green onions, chopped

¼ tsp. minced garlic

1 tsp. sugar

2 cross-section slices of jalapeño pepper

INSTRUCTIONS

1. Wash hands.
2. Place ingredients in a blender and combine well.
3. Refrigerate one hour.
4. Goes well with pulled pork burritos, salads, or any other desired dish.

Pairs well with Cafe Rio Pulled Pork (pg 95).

Tip: You can eliminate the jalapeño pepper for a mild sauce to use with many different dishes.

Recipe courtesy of Robin Hoelzle

TURKEY, BLACK BEAN & ORZO SALAD

Serving size: ½ cup • Serves: 6

NUTRITIONAL INFORMATION (given for whole recipe)
Calories: 232 kcals • Carbohydrates: 27 g • Protein: 24 g • Fat: 3 g

QUICK AND EASY   HIGH PROTEIN   HIGH FIBER

INGREDIENTS

¼ pound orzo pasta

¼ whole turkey breast poached and cut into bite-sized pieces (about 3 slices)

½ medium red onion, chopped fine

1 yellow bell pepper, chopped fine

1 (15-oz.) can black beans, rinsed and drained

2½ Tbsp. chopped coriander

INSTRUCTIONS

1. Wash hands.
2. Prepare orzo according to package directions.
3. Toss all the ingredients together to serve.

The beans add a punch of protein and fiber.

Tip: A great way to use leftover thanksgiving turkey.

Variation tip: Use different colored bell peppers for added color and micronutrients.

Variation tip: Can add tomatoes, avocado, or additional bell pepper for added fiber and micronutrients.

Recipe courtesy of Tamsin Barlow

QUINOA SALAD WITH AVOCADOS & BLACK BEANS

Serving size: ¾ cup • Serves: 8

NUTRITIONAL INFORMATION

Calories: 243 kcals • Carbohydrates: 37 g • Protein: 9 g • Fat: 8 g

VEGETARIAN/VEGAN QUICK AND EASY HIGH FIBER MAKE ONCE EAT TWICE

INGREDIENTS

1 Tbsp. olive or coconut oil

1 cup dry quinoa, rinsed

1½-2 cup water

½ tsp. minced garlic

1 can black beans, drained and rinsed

1 avocado, chopped into chunks

handful of cherry tomatoes, quartered

1 can corn, drained

1 red bell pepper, chopped into chunks

½ bunch cilantro, diced

1 lime, juiced

½-1 tsp. cumin

1-1½ tsp. olive oil

salt to taste

INSTRUCTIONS

1. Wash hands.
2. Warm oil in a medium saucepan over medium heat.
3. Once the oil is hot, add rinsed quinoa and toast for about 2-3 minutes until it starts smelling nutty.
4. Add water and garlic. Stir once. Cover and simmer with lid on for 20 minutes.
5. While the quinoa is cooking, prepare the other ingredients to be combined together.
6. For dressing: combine lime juice, oil, cumin, and salt. Whisk aggressively. Adjust seasoning to taste.
7. When quinoa has finished, remove from heat and fluff with a fork. Add to black beans and toss to warm them through.
8. Let quinoa cool for about 5 minutes and then add remaining ingredients, including dressing. Mix together.
9. Serve with tortillas, chips, or any other desired topping.

Quinoa is a great, underappreciated food. Filled with fiber, protein, and micronutrients, it adds not only variety to your meal plan but also nutrients for your body.

Storage tip: This is a great recipe to make at the beginning of the week to meal prep and use for a quick and healthy meal or side during the week. It stores well in the fridge for up to 1 week.

Nutrition tip: The avocado provides a great boost of healthy fats.

Use leftover cherry tomatoes to make Lemon Pesto Chicken with Asparagus and Tomatoes (pg 64).

STRAWBERRY SALAD WITH POPPYSEED DRESSING

Serving size: ½ cup • Serves: 8

NUTRITIONAL INFORMATION
Calories: 56 kcals • Carbohydrates: 8 g • Protein: 1 g • Fat: 3 g

QUICK AND EASY

INGREDIENTS

1 Tbsp. sugar

2 Tbsp. light mayonnaise

1 Tbsp. skim milk

1 Tbsp. poppy seeds

1 Tbsp. vinegar

10-oz. bag romaine lettuce, roughly chopped

1 cup sliced strawberries

1 Tbsp. toasted slivered almonds

INSTRUCTIONS

1. Wash hands.
2. Combine sugar, mayonnaise, milk, poppy seeds, and vinegar in a small bowl. Whisk to combine well.
3. Place lettuce, strawberries, and almonds in a large bowl. Add dressing and toss lightly.

A great summer meal during strawberry season.

Variation tip: Make a mixed berry salad by adding fresh raspberries, blueberries, or blackberries.

Variation tip: You can use spinach in place of or in addition to lettuce to boost your protein and iron intake.

Use leftover strawberries to make Strawberry Trifle (pg 174) and extra almonds to make Banana Oat Chewies (pg 158) or Fruit Crisp (pg 166).

Recipe courtesy of Jodee Thomas

THAI CHICKEN SALAD

Serving size: ½ cup • Serves: 4

NUTRITIONAL INFORMATION

Calories: 293 kcals • Carbohydrates: 29 g • Protein: 18 g • Fat: 13 g

MAKE AHEAD QUICK AND EASY

INGREDIENTS

½ pound linguine

½ tsp. olive oil

½ pound cooked and shredded chicken

1 bunch green onions, sliced

½ bunch fresh cilantro, chopped

1 fresh jalapeño, seeded and minced

½ pound snow peas, thinly sliced

¼ cup low-sodium soy sauce

2 Tbsp. creamy peanut butter

2 Tbsp. rice vinegar

1 Tbsp. sugar

2 Tbsp. sesame oil

INSTRUCTIONS

1. Wash hands.
2. Cook linguine in salted water according to package directions. Drain and rinse in cold water. Drain again and put in a large bowl. Toss with oil.
3. Add chicken, green onions, cilantro, jalapeños, and snow peas. Mix well.
4. For dressing, blend soy sauce, peanut butter, vinegar, sugar, and sesame oil in the blender. Pour over salad and mix well.
5. Can be made ahead or served immediately.
6. For some extra heat, use chili sesame oil (optional).

A great way to get a full meal in one bowl.

Use other half pound of linguine to make Salmon Zucchini Linguine (pg 44) and extra peanut butter to make Nice Cream (pg 178).

Recipe courtesy of Jolene Reed

MEXICAN BLACK BEAN SALAD

Serving size: ½ cup • Serves: 12

NUTRITIONAL INFORMATION

Calories: 174 kcals • Carbohydrates: 16 g • Protein: 4 g • Fat: 12 g

MAKE AHEAD · QUICK AND EASY · VEGETARIAN/VEGAN · HIGH FIBER · MAKE ONCE EAT TWICE · GREAT FOR A PARTY

INGREDIENTS

1 lime

½ cup olive oil

½ tsp. minced garlic

1 tsp. salt

¼ tsp. cayenne pepper

1 can black beans, drained and rinsed

1½ cups frozen corn kernels, thawed

1 avocado, diced

1 red bell pepper, chopped

2 tomatoes, chopped

6 green onions, chopped

¼ cup cilantro, chopped

INSTRUCTIONS

1. Wash hands.
2. Mix lime juice, olive oil, garlic, salt, and cayenne pepper in a small container and refrigerate.
3. Combine beans, corn, avocado, bell pepper, tomatoes, green onions, and cilantro.
4. Shake lime dressing and pour over salad. Stir well and serve.

Variation tip: Add ¼ tsp. cayenne pepper for some spice.

This is packed with veggies and beans—a great boost to protein, fiber, vitamins, and minerals.

Use leftover frozen corn to make Arroz con Pollo (pg 50) or Black Bean Salsa (pg 102).

BREAD

/bred/ (*noun*)

food made of flour, water, and yeast or another leavening agent, mixed together and baked.

OLIVE OIL PIZZA DOUGH

Serving size: 1 9–inch crust • Serves: 1 crust

NUTRITIONAL INFORMATION (per slice, 12 slices per pizza)
Calories: 87 kcals • Carbohydrates: 16 g • Protein: 2 g • Fat: 2 g

VEGETARIAN/VEGAN BUDGET SAVER

INGREDIENTS

1 cup lukewarm water

1⅓ Tbsp. extra virgin olive oil

1 ½ tsp. granulated yeast

1 tsp. sugar

2¼ cups unbleached all-purpose flour

1½ tsp. coarse ground kosher salt

INSTRUCTIONS

1. Wash hands.
2. Preheat oven to 450 degrees.
3. Combine water, olive oil, yeast, and sugar. Mix together and let sit about 10 minutes.
4. Add flour and salt, mix dough thoroughly together. Add additional flour as needed.
5. Roll out dough into a circle and spread any desired toppings/spices on top.
6. Bake for 15-20 minutes, or until golden brown and cooked through.

A great way to make eating "in" as tasty as delivery!

Works well for pizza, focaccia, olive bread, or other dishes.

Variation tip: Add some pizzazz to the crust by blending in some spices. Italian seasoning, garlic powder and parsley, or some Parmesan cheese can give an extra kick to the crust.

ARTISAN BREADS

Serving size: 1 slice (each loaf yields about 16 slices) • Serves: 16–32

NUTRITIONAL INFORMATION (per 16 slices)
Calories: 83 kcals • Carbohydrates: 18 g • Protein: 3 g • Fat: 0 g

PREP TIME REQUIRED   VEGETARIAN/VEGAN   SERVES A CROWD

INGREDIENTS

1½ cups lukewarm water

2¼ tsp. granulated yeast

2¼ tsp. coarse ground kosher salt

3¼ cups unbleached all-purpose flour

Tip: Make the dough starter ahead of time. Keep in the fridge to use later for a fast loaf.

Variation tip: You can do different flavors from one starter. Try cinnamon swirl by mixing in some cinnamon and sugar to the loaf when preparing to bake it. Or add some herbs and spices to give it a different flavor.

MIXING INSTRUCTIONS

1. Wash hands.
2. In a large bowl, pour in water and add yeast and salt. Let sit for several minutes. Pour in flour and stir by hand or mix with an electric mixer until all of the flour is incorporated into the dough. This will be a wet dough.
3. Put the lid on the container, but do not snap it shut. You want the gases from the yeast to escape (put a little hole in the top of the lid so you can close the lid and still allow the gases to get out). Let rest at room temperature about 2 hours, or until dough rises and collapses. Do not punch down or knead. The dough should be flat on top, and some of the bubbles may even appear to be popping.
4. Put the lid on the container and refrigerate for at least 3 hours. This dough can be stored in the fridge and used for 10 days.

BAKING INSTRUCTIONS

5. Preheat oven to 450 degrees 30 minutes before baking time with baking stone on middle rack and empty broiler tray on the bottom of oven.
6. Dust surface or refrigerated dough with flour and cut off 1 pound (¼ dough, or about a grapefruit size) piece. Dust with more flour and quickly shape into a ball by stretching the surface around to the bottom on all 4 sides, rotating the ball ¼ turn as you go.
7. Allow loaf to rest, loosely covered, on parchment paper for 90-120 minutes (or 40 minutes if using fresh, un-refrigerated dough).
8. Just before baking, use pastry brush to paint the top of the loaf with water or dust with flour. Slice loaf with ¼-inch deep parallel cuts, or however desired.
9. Place parchment paper with loaf on stone in oven. Quickly pour 1 cup hot tap water into broiler tray and close oven door.
10. Bake for 35-40 minutes (or for rolls, bake for 20-25 minutes) until loaf is richly browned and firm.

OATMEAL BREAD

Serving size: 1 9x5 loaf • Serves: 12

NUTRITIONAL INFORMATION (per slice, 12 slices per loaf)
Calories: 155 kcals • Carbohydrates: 27 g • Protein: 5 g • Fat: 3 g

PREP TIME REQUIRED · VEGETARIAN/VEGAN · HIGH FIBER

INGREDIENTS

1⅓ cups lukewarm water

2 tsp. dry active yeast

2 Tbsp. sugar

2 Tbsp. oil

3 cups flour (I use 2 cups all-purpose, 1 cup whole wheat)

1 cup rolled oats

1½ tsp. salt

INSTRUCTIONS

1. Wash hands.
2. In a large mixing bowl (or standing mixer with bread paddle), combine water, yeast, sugar, and oil. Allow to rest 10 minutes. Add flour, oats, and salt. Mix thoroughly. Then knead by hand (about 10 minutes) or with a standing mixer (about 5 minutes.)
3. Cover the bowl with a dish towel or plastic wrap. Let rise for 90 minutes. Punch down the dough, and knead by hand, turning the dough over on itself several times.
4. Coat a 9x5 bread pan with non-stick cooking spray.
5. Shape the dough into a loaf and place it in the pan. Cover with a dish towel, and let rise 30 more minutes, until it has risen 1-2 inches above the pan.
6. While the dough is rising in the pan, pre-heat oven to 375 degrees.
7. Place the pan in the oven and bake for 25-30 minutes, until golden brown.
8. Remove loaf from oven and pan. Let bread cool on a cooling rack or dish towel. Allow to cool at least 10 minutes before cutting. Serve as desired.

Tip: The oatmeal in this bread boosts the fiber in your diet. Plus it makes great-tasting toast for a quick breakfast on the run.

Tip: Great to pair with homemade Hot Cocoa (pg 192) for a warm breakfast on a cold morning.

Recipe courtesy of Pennies and Pancakes

OATMEAL PUMPKIN BREAD

Serving size: 3 loaves (yields about 12 slices per loaf) • Serves: 36

NUTRITIONAL INFORMATION (per slice, 12 slices per loaf)
Calories: 96 kcals • Carbohydrates: 18 g • Protein: 2 g • Fat: 2 g

VEGETARIAN/VEGAN HIGH FIBER SERVES A CROWD

INGREDIENTS

- 2 cups lukewarm water
- 1 cup pumpkin puree
- ⅓ cup honey
- 5 Tbsp. unsalted butter, melted
- 1½ Tbsp. granulated yeast
- 1½ Tbsp. coarse ground kosher salt
- 4 cups unbleached all-purpose flour
- ¾ cup whole wheat flour
- ¾ cup rye flour
- ½ cup old fashioned oats

INSTRUCTIONS

1. Wash hands.
2. Preheat oven to 375 degrees.
3. Combine all ingredients and mix together well. Add additional flour if needed.
4. Pour into greased bread pans. Brush each loaf with water and slash before baking.
5. Bake for 40–45 minutes.

Tip: This is not the sweet bread that comes out every fall. It's a great tasting traditional style of bread, packed with vitamin A from the pumpkin puree.

Use extra pumpkin to make Pumpkin Pancakes (pg 40) or Pumpkin Muffins (pg 161).

CORNBREAD

Serving size: 1 (2–inch) square • Serves: 16 • Yields: 1 9x9 pan

NUTRITIONAL INFORMATION

Calories: 115 kcals • Carbohydrates: 15 g • Protein: 2 g • Fat: 5 g

QUICK AND EASY VEGETARIAN/VEGAN MAKE ONCE EAT TWICE

INGREDIENTS

1 cup cornmeal

1 cup flour

½ cup sugar

4 tsp. baking powder

¾ tsp. salt

⅓ cup olive oil

2 eggs, beaten

1 cup milk

INSTRUCTIONS

1. Wash hands.
2. Preheat oven to 400 degrees.
3. In a medium bowl, mix together cornmeal, flour, sugar, baking powder, and salt.
4. Add oil, beaten eggs, and milk. Mix together using a hand mixer or whisk until smooth and no lumps remain.
5. Pour mixture into a greased baking dish. For an 8x8 baking dish, bake 22-25 minutes; a 9x9 dish, 20-23 minutes; a muffin tin, 17-18 minutes.
6. Serve immediately with butter or honey, or as a side with chili or any other desired dish.
7. Store in the fridge for up to 3 days.

Pairs well with Best Crockpot Chili (pg 105) for a great chili/cornbread combo.
Use leftovers for a fruity breakfast, pairing with whipped cream and strawberries.
Variation tip: Use whole wheat flour for a boost of fiber.

BREADSTICKS

Serving size: 1 (6–inch) breadstick • Serves: 6, varies depending on size desired

NUTRITIONAL INFORMATION (per 1 breadstick)
Calories: 185 kcals • Carbohydrates: 24 g • Protein: 4 g • Fat: 8 g

QUICK AND EASY · VEGETARIAN/VEGAN · MAKE ONCE EAT TWICE

INGREDIENTS

1½ tsp. yeast

¾ cup warm water

1 Tbsp. sugar

¼ tsp. salt

1½ cups flour

2 Tbsp. butter, melted

garlic salt (to taste)

Parmesan cheese (to taste)

Italian seasoning (to taste)

INSTRUCTIONS

1. Wash hands.
2. Preheat oven to 375 degrees.
3. Dissolve yeast in warm water. Add sugar and let sit for 5 minutes.
4. Add salt and mix together. Add flour. Knead for 3 minutes while adding a little more flour as needed (the stickier the better).
5. Pour half the butter into a 9x13 pan.
6. Pat the dough into a 6x6-inch square. Slice the dough into ½-inch sticks and place each stick in the pan and brush each breadstick with the rest of the butter.
7. Sprinkle with garlic salt, Parmesan cheese, and Italian seasoning.
8. Let breadsticks rise for 30 minutes. Bake for 15-20 minutes or until golden brown.

Pairs well with Chicken Alfredo (pg 55), Minestrone Soup (pg 114), or Creamy Parmesan and Bacon Pasta (pg 91).

Recipe courtesy of Paige Larsen

PRETZELS

Serving size: 1 medium pretzel • Serves: 9, varies depending on size

NUTRITIONAL INFORMATION (per pretzel)
Calories: 96 kcals • Carbohydrates: 20 g • Protein: 4 g • Fat: 0 g

VEGETARIAN/VEGAN BUDGET SAVER GREAT FOR A PARTY

INGREDIENTS

1½ tsp. yeast

¾ cups warm water

1½ tsp. sugar

½ tsp. salt

2 cups flour

1 egg, beaten

Kosher salt (to taste)

INSTRUCTIONS

1. Wash hands.
2. Preheat oven to 425 degrees.
3. Dissolve yeast and water. Add sugar. Add salt after about 30 seconds.
4. Blend in flour and knead until smooth.
5. Cut into medium pieces. Roll, twist, and shape into desired position.
6. Placed on a greased cookie sheet. Brush with beaten egg and sprinkle with kosher salt.
7. Bake for 12–15 minutes, until golden brown.

Variation tip: You can do different flavors as toppings. Cinnamon and sugar, kosher salt, or Parmesan and basil all pair well to give different tastes to the same base recipe.

Recipe courtesy of Pat Baker

DESSERT

des·sert *(noun)*

the sweet course eaten at the end of a meal.

TRES LECHES

Serving size: 1 (2–inch) square • Serves: 9 • Yields: 1 9x13 pan

NUTRITIONAL INFORMATION

Calories: 275 kcals • Carbohydrates: 50 g • Protein: 5 g • Fat: 6 g

MAKE AHEAD PREP TIME REQUIRED VEGETARIAN/VEGAN

DESSERT

INGREDIENTS

1 yellow cake mix

1 (5-oz.) can evaporated milk

1 small can condensed milk

1 cup milk

2 cups whipped cream (or desired amount to top cake)

INSTRUCTIONS

1. Wash hands.
2. Prepare yellow cake mixture according to box instructions and place in a 9x13 pan. Bake according to instructions.
3. After the cake is baked, poke holes in it with a fork. Be careful not to destroy it. Puncture it enough to allow the liquid to absorb.
4. In a separate bowl, mix the 3 milks until well blended and pour over the cake.
5. Put the cake in the fridge for a few hours (the longer the better). Just before serving, top with whipped cream.

BANANA OAT CHEWIES

Serving size: 1 (4–inch chewie) • Serves: 8

NUTRITIONAL INFORMATION (per bar)
Calories: 56 kcals • Carbohydrates: 11 g • Protein: 1 g • Fat: 1 g

VEGETARIAN/VEGAN HIGH FIBER MAKE ONCE EAT TWICE

INGREDIENTS

1 large (or 2 small) very ripe bananas, mashed

4 tsp. honey

⅔ cup whole rolled oats

4 tsp. slivered almonds

¼ tsp. salt

½ tsp. cinnamon

1 Tbsp. vegan chocolate chips (Ghirardelli or similar)

¼ cup dried fruit, nuts, or seeds (optional)

INSTRUCTIONS

1. Wash hands.
2. Preheat oven to 350 degrees.
3. Using a potato masher, mash bananas in a medium-sized mixing bowl. Add honey and stir to combine.
4. Add oats, almonds, salt, cinnamon, and chocolate chips. Mix thoroughly until well incorporated.
5. Lightly coat a 9x13 baking pan with non-stick cooking spray. Press banana-oat mixture evenly into the pan.
6. Bake for 18–20 minutes.
7. Remove from oven. Cut into 8 portions. Remove from pan and allow to cool completely on a cooling rack to avoid soggy bottoms.
8. Store in an airtight container on the counter or in the refrigerator for up to 1 week.

Nutrition tip: This recipe provides a sweet treat but is a great source of fiber from the rolled oats, potassium and other nutrients from the bananas, and healthy fats from the almonds.

Use any leftover ripe bananas to make Nice Cream (pg 178).

Recipe courtesy of Pennies and Pancakes

PUMPKIN MUFFINS

Serving size: 1 muffin • Serves: 24

NUTRITIONAL INFORMATION

Calories: 77 kcals • Carbohydrates: 16 g • Protein: 1 g • Fat: 1 g

QUICK AND EASY · VEGETARIAN/VEGAN · SERVES A CROWD · MAKE ONCE EAT TWICE

INGREDIENTS

1 (15-oz.) can puréed pumpkin

1 box cake mix (yellow or white)

1 Tbsp. pumpkin pie spice

¼ cup water

1 bag chocolate chips (optional)

INSTRUCTIONS

1. Wash hands.
2. Preheat oven to 350 degrees and spray 24 muffin tins with cooking spray.
3. Pour pumpkin, cake mix, pie spice, and water into mixing bowl and combine with a mixer until well blended (you may need to add a little more water).
4. Fold in chocolate chips (optional).
5. Scoop into muffin tins and bake at 350 for 18–20 minutes.
6. Serve warm or cool.

A great alternative to traditional cupcakes, these are sweet enough to curb the sweet craving but loaded with vitamins and minerals from the pumpkin to help boost your health.

If you use a larger can of pumpkin, use the extra pumpkin to make Pumpkin Pancakes (pg 40) or Oatmeal Pumpkin Bread (pg 147).

CARROT CUPCAKES

Serving size: 1 cupcake • Serves: 8

NUTRITIONAL INFORMATION

Calories: 137 kcals • Carbohydrates: 23 g • Protein: 3 g • Fat: 4 g

VEGETARIAN/VEGAN HIGH FIBER VARIATION ON TRADITIONAL RECIPE

INGREDIENTS

½ cup sugar

⅓ cup puréed pinto beans (or any other type beans)

1¾ Tbsp. olive oil

2 eggs (or 1 eggs and 2 egg whites)

⅔ cups flour

½ tsp. baking soda

¼ tsp. salt

1 tsp. cinnamon

1-2 cups carrots, finely grated

INSTRUCTIONS

1. Wash hands.
2. Preheat oven to 350 degrees.
3. In a large bowl, mix sugar, puréed beans, oil, and eggs together.
4. In a separate bowl, combine flour, soda, salt, and cinnamon. Stir dry ingredients into the wet mixture.
5. Fold in carrots.
6. Spoon into well-greased muffin tins, filling about ½-⅔ of the tin.
7. Bake for 16 minutes (for mini cupcakes) or 18-20 minutes for regular cupcakes.
8. Frost with cream cheese frosting (optional).

The hidden ingredients in these cupcakes make them a great substitute for the traditional recipe. This version boosts the protein and fiber while decreasing the fat and calories. You can finally have your cupcake and eat it too.

Variation tip: The type of carrot shavings is up to you—you can chop them extra fine or grate big pieces. Follow your personal preference.

The vitamin A from the carrots helps boost your eyesight, especially at night.

Use leftover bean puree to make Low-Fat Whole Wheat Blueberry Muffins (pg 39).

BUTTERSCOTCH OATMEAL COOKIES

Serving size: 1 cookie • Serves: 12

NUTRITIONAL INFORMATION

Calories: 212 kcals • Carbohydrates: 39 g • Protein: 3 g • Fat: 6 g

VEGETARIAN/VEGAN HIGH FIBER

DESSERT

INGREDIENTS

½ cup applesauce

½ cup packed brown sugar

¼ cup white sugar

1 egg

½ tsp. vanilla

¾ cup quick oats

¾ cup flour

½ tsp. baking soda

½ tsp. salt

1½ tsp. cinnamon

¼ tsp. nutmeg (optional)

1 cup butterscotch chips

INSTRUCTIONS

1. Wash hands.
2. Preheat oven to 350 degrees.
3. Beat applesauce and sugars until well blended. Beat in egg and vanilla.
4. Add dry ingredients and mix well. Fold in butterscotch chips.
5. Drop in rounded spoonfuls onto a cookie sheet. Bake 8–10 minutes, or until done.

These cookies are so good, you'll never know they are low sugar and boosted with fiber from the oatmeal.

Storage tip: Put the bag of butterscotch chips in a sealed bag in the freezer and use them in the future to make more cookies.

DESSERT

FRUIT CRISP

Serving size: ½ cup • Serves: 6

NUTRITIONAL INFORMATION

Calories: 129 kcals • Carbohydrates: 24 g • Protein: 1 g • Fat: 4 g

VEGETARIAN/VEGAN

INGREDIENTS

Fruit mixture

3 cups fruit, cut into medium pieces (suggested combos: pears and blackberries, apples and cranberries, apples and raspberries–whatever is desired)

½ cup sugar

2 Tbsp. cornstarch (add more for more watery fruits–between ⅓ and ½ cup)

¼ tsp. salt

¼ tsp. cinnamon

Topping

¼ cup all-purpose flour

2 Tbsp. brown sugar, packed

2 Tbsp. sugar

¼ tsp. cinnamon

pinch of salt

2 Tbsp. cold unsalted butter, cut in pieces

2 ½ Tbsp. rolled oats or sliced almonds

INSTRUCTIONS

1. Wash hands.
2. Preheat oven to 350 degrees.
3. Mix together fruit, sugar, cornstarch, salt, and cinnamon. Place mixture in a 9x9 greased cake pan.
4. Mix topping ingredients together by blending dry ingredients and then adding butter and mixing well until it resembles a coarse meal.
5. Top fruit with topping mixture. Bake 35-40 minutes until the juices in the middle are bubbling.

Variation tip: Buying fruits in season not only gives variety to this recipe, but it also keeps the cost low.

Tip: Use canned fruit if fresh isn't available.

Recipe courtesy of Melanie Filmore

YOGURT POPSICLES

Serving size: 1 popsicle • Serves: 6

NUTRITIONAL INFORMATION
Calories: 93 kcals • Carbohydrates: 16 g • Protein: 4 g • Fat: 1 g

MAKE AHEAD | PREP TIME REQUIRED | QUICK AND EASY | VEGETARIAN/VEGAN

INGREDIENTS

2 cups yogurt

2 Tbsp. frozen orange juice concentrate

¼ cup sugar

½ tsp. vanilla

INSTRUCTIONS

1. Wash hands.
2. Combine ingredients well. Pour into popsicle molds (or 3-oz. paper cups).
3. Freeze until almost firm and insert wooden sticks.
4. Complete the freezing until solid.

A great way to beat the heat and boost your calcium.

Substitution tip: Use Greek yogurt for an added boost of protein.

Use leftover frozen orange juice concentrate to make Orange Julius (pg 24).

RICE PUDDING

Serving size: ½ cup • Serves: 8

NUTRITIONAL INFORMATION

Calories: 326 kcals • Carbohydrates: 58 g • Protein: 10 g • Fat: 6 g

MAKE AHEAD QUICK AND EASY BUDGET SAVER GREAT FOR A PARTY

INGREDIENTS

2½ cups cooked rice

3 cups skim milk

14 oz. sweetened condensed milk

2 tsp. cinnamon (or two cinnamon sticks)

½ tsp. salt (optional)

1 tsp. vanilla

INSTRUCTIONS

1. Wash hands.
2. Place rice, milk, condensed milk, cinnamon, and salt into a medium-sized pot.
3. Heat to boil, stirring constantly.
4. Reduce heat and simmer, continuing to stir until mixture thickens (keep in mind, it will continue to thicken more as it cools).
5. Remove from heat. If using cinnamon sticks, remove them.
6. Add vanilla and stir.
7. Serve warm or cold.

Tip: A great way to use leftover rice from a different meal.

Substitution tip: Use brown rice for added fiber.

Use leftover rice for Cilantro Lime Rice (pg 181).

SLOW COOKER FUDGE CAKE

Serving size: ½ cup • Serves: 8

NUTRITIONAL INFORMATION

Calories: 422 kcals • Carbohydrates: 84 g • Protein: 6 g • Fat: 16 g

SLOW COOKER   VEGETARIAN/VEGAN

INGREDIENTS

1 cup brown sugar, divided

½ cup flour

3 Tbsp. cocoa, divided

1 tsp. baking powder

¼ tsp. salt

¼ cup milk

1 Tbsp. butter, melted

¼ tsp. vanilla

¾ cups semisweet chocolate chips

1 cup boiling water

INSTRUCTIONS

1. Wash hands.
2. Turn slow cooker on to high and coat with cooking spray.
3. Combine ½ cup brown sugar, flour, 1 Tbsp. cocoa, baking powder, and salt in a bowl. Mix together well.
4. Add milk, butter, and vanilla. Mix thoroughly.
5. Spread mixture into the slow cooker. Sprinkle with chocolate chips.
6. In another bowl, combine remaining brown sugar and cocoa. Stir in boiling water. Pour over batter. DO NOT STIR. Cover and cook for 4 hours.
7. Check with a toothpick to determine doneness. Serve with ice cream or any other desired side.

A little goes a long way. Small servings are the way to go. The chocolate is very rich and will surely satisfy any gotta-get-some-chocolate craving in a couple of spoonfuls.

Use leftover chocolate chips to make Banana Oat Chewies (pg 158).

STRAWBERRY TRIFLE

Serving size: ½ cup • Serves: 20

NUTRITIONAL INFORMATION

Calories: 82 kcals • Carbohydrates: 14 g • Protein: 1 g • Fat: 1 g

MAKE AHEAD · QUICK AND EASY · SERVES A CROWD · GREAT FOR A PARTY

INGREDIENTS

1 pound strawberries, washed and sliced (if doing option of circling strawberries around the outside, will need ½ pound more)

1 large tub Cool Whip

1 large package vanilla instant pudding, mixed with 3 cups milk (according to package directions)

1 large angel food cake, cut into cubes

INSTRUCTIONS

1. Wash hands.
2. In a small-medium glass bowl, place a layer of angel food cake cubes (use almost ½).
3. Spread almost ½ of the strawberries over the cake. You can circle strawberry slices around the outside of the bowl for a pretty design (optional).
4. Pour almost ½ of the pudding over and spread around.
5. Spoon Cool Whip over, and spread until all pudding is covered.
6. Repeat layering process.
7. Top with remaining strawberries and angel food cake cubes in any design.
8. Dollop Cool Whip on top.
9. Chill until ready to serve.

Tip: Add blueberries for a festive Fourth of July dessert.

Tip: Use banana pudding in place of vanilla pudding.

Tip: Make in single serving sizes for individual desserts.

Variation idea: Use chocolate pudding, brownies, and cool whip. Cut the brownies into small pieces, and layer the same.

Use leftover strawberries for Strawberry Salad with Poppyseed Dressing (pg 134) or Fruit Crisp (pg 133).

CHOCOLATE LASAGNA

Serving size: ¼ cup • Serves: 6

NUTRITIONAL INFORMATION
Calories: 80 kcals • Carbohydrates: 15 g • Protein: 2 g • Fat: 2 g

MAKE AHEAD PREP TIME REQUIRED VARIATION ON TRADITIONAL RECIPE

INGREDIENTS

18 regular Oreo cookies
3 Tbsp. butter, melted
4 oz. cream cheese, softened
2 Tbsp. sugar
3¾ cups cold milk
6 oz. Cool Whip (½ tub)
1 (3.9-oz.) package chocolate instant pudding
¾ cup mini chocolate chips

INSTRUCTIONS

1. Wash hands.
2. Crush Oreos finely (use food processor or do it by hand).
3. Place Oreo crumbs in a large bowl and stir in 3 Tbsp. melted butter with a fork. Mix together well.
4. Transfer crumbs to a 9x13 pan and press into the bottom. Put the pan in the fridge.
5. Meanwhile, mix cream cheese with a mixer until light and fluffy. Add sugar and cold milk. Mix well.
6. Stir in ¾ cup Cool Whip and then spread the mixture over the cookie crust in the pan.
7. In a separate bowl, mix the chocolate pudding and milk. Whisk together until it starts to thicken. Spread over cream cheese layer.
8. Let set for 5 minutes. Spread the remainder of the Cool Whip over the top. Sprinkle with chocolate chips.
9. Place in the freezer for 1 hour or fridge for 4 hours before serving.

Use leftover Cool Whip to make Fruit Dip (pg 11).

NICE CREAM

Serving size: ½ cup • Serves: 4

NUTRITIONAL INFORMATION

Calories: 252 kcals • Carbohydrates: 29 g • Protein: 7 g • Fat: 12 g

QUICK AND EASY | VEGETARIAN/VEGAN | HIGH FIBER | BUDGET SAVER | VARIATION ON TRADITIONAL RECIPE

INGREDIENTS

4 medium ripe bananas, cut into chunks and frozen (freeze for at least 2 hours)

4 Tbsp. peanut butter (with no added sugar, if desired)

4 Tbsp. unsweetened cocoa powder

1 tsp. pure vanilla extract

4 Tbsp. chopped peanuts

INSTRUCTIONS

1. Place bananas in a large food processor.
2. Add peanut butter, cocoa powder, and vanilla.
3. Blend until smooth, about 2 to 3 minutes.
4. Transfer to serving bowls and garnish with peanuts. Serve immediately.

A smart way to use up overripe bananas.

A great way to get some fiber and protein in your dessert!

Variation: Blend bananas with strawberries for a fruity nice cream.

Variation tip: This recipe is very versatile. Use any kind of frozen fruit for different flavors.

Use leftover bananas to make Banana Oat Chewies (pg 158).

Recipe courtesy of Elizabeth Ward www.betteristhenewperfect.com

SIDES

/sid/ (*noun*)

a dish served as subsidiary to the main one.

CILANTRO LIME RICE

SIDES

Serving size: ½ cup • Serves: 4

NUTRITIONAL INFORMATION

Calories: 45 kcals • Carbohydrates: 6 g • Protein: 1 g • Fat: 2 g

QUICK AND EASY   MAKE ONCE EAT TWICE

INGREDIENTS

1½ tsp. olive oil

½ cup basmati rice (or any type you have on hand)

1 clove garlic, minced (or ½ tsp. jarred)

¾ cup chicken broth (if using regular rice, up chicken broth to 1 cup)

juice from ½ fresh lime juice

¼ cup cilantro, chopped

½ tsp. salt

INSTRUCTIONS

1. Wash hands.
2. Add oil to saucepan and heat on low. Add rice and garlic. Sauté for 2 minutes on medium heat, stirring frequently.
3. Add chicken broth, lime juice, and salt. Bring to a boil.
4. Cover and simmer on low for 15 minutes or according to rice package directions.
5. When rice is done, add chopped cilantro and stir to mix in.

Substitution tip: Use brown rice for added fiber.

Use other half of the lime to make Mango Salsa (pg 22) or Teriyaki Flank Steak (pg 85).

Pairs well with Cafe Rio Pulled Pork (pg 95) and Black Bean Salsa (pg 102).

Recipe courtesy of Kami Quist

POTATO WEDGES

Serving size: 5–6 wedges • Serves: 4–6

NUTRITIONAL INFORMATION

Calories: 135 kcals • Carbohydrates: 24 g • Protein: 3 g • Fat: 3 g

VEGETARIAN/VEGAN

INGREDIENTS

3-4 medium potatoes

1 Tbsp. olive oil

½ tsp. garlic salt

½ tsp. garlic powder

1 tsp. onion powder

Optional ingredients (for different variations)

chili powder (to taste)

cayenne pepper (to taste)

chives (to taste)

dried parsley (to taste)

grated Parmesan cheese

INSTRUCTIONS

1. Wash hands.
2. Preheat oven to 375 degrees.
3. Scrub potatoes and rinse under cold water. Pat dry.
4. Cut potatoes into wedges or thin steak fries (about 6-8 wedges per potato).
5. Using a large mixing bowl, toss potatoes in oil.
6. In a small bowl, mix dry ingredients thoroughly. Pour over potatoes and toss to coat.
7. Spread potatoes in a single layer on an oiled baking sheet. Bake for 30-35 minutes, or until potatoes are tender. Test with a fork. Sprinkle with salt to taste.

Potatoes are a great way to get fiber, vitamin C, potassium, and antioxidants, just to name a few!

Use leftover potatoes to make Make It Easy Chicken (pg 67), Stew (pg 86), or Zuppa Toscana (pg 122).

Recipe courtesy of Pennies and Pancakes

AMAZING FRIED RICE

Serving size: 1 cup • Serves: 4

NUTRITIONAL INFORMATION

Calories: 181 kcals • Carbohydrates: 25 g • Protein: 8 g • Fat: 6 g

HIGH FIBER MAKE ONCE EAT TWICE

INGREDIENTS

1½ cups cold cooked rice

1 Tbsp. vegetable oil

¼-½ cup ham, diced (depending on amount desired)

½ small onion, diced

½ tsp. jarred minced garlic (or 1 fresh clove, minced)

2 medium carrots, peeled and diced (can add more)

½ small head broccoli, stem discarded and florets chopped

1 egg

2 Tbsp. low-sodium soy sauce

INSTRUCTIONS

1. Wash hands.
2. Make sure rice has been cooked and refrigerated.
3. Heat oil in a large skillet over medium-high heat. Add ham and cook until lightly browned, stirring occasionally.
4. Add onion. Cook for about 2 minutes, until the onion is fragrant. Add garlic and cook an additional 30 seconds or so.
5. Add remaining vegetables and cook for 3 minutes, stirring occasionally.
6. Push the ham and vegetables to the sides of the skillet with your spoon. Add the egg, scramble it, and incorporate it with the ham and vegetables.
7. Add rice and stir everything together. Add soy sauce and stir until rice is hot and everything is mixed together. Serve immediately.

Preparation tip: 1 cup dry long-grain rice yields 3 cups cooked.

Preparation tip: This fried rice is a little stickier than restaurant-style fried rice because it uses oil for frying and contains an over-abundance of vegetables. If you're not a fan of sticky rice, use pre-cooked cold rice to combat the stickiness.

Tip: A great way to use leftover rice.

Tip: This recipe is versatile. Different vegetables or varieties of rice or meat may be substituted: brown rice, basmati rice, jasmine rice, corn, peas, mushrooms, peppers, chicken, shrimp, beef—whatever you have in your fridge that needs to be used up

Use leftover rice to make Rice Pudding (pg 170) and use leftover ham to make Eggs Benedict (pg 36) or Chicken Cordon Bleu (pg 56).

MAC & CHEESE

Serving size: 1 cup • Serves: 10

NUTRITIONAL INFORMATION (for total recipe – need to divide out with servings)
Calories: 385 kcals • Carbohydrates: 42 g • Protein: 14 g • Fat: 12 g

VEGETARIAN/VEGAN SERVES A CROWD

INGREDIENTS

1 box elbow macaroni noodles

½ cup butter or margarine

½ cup flour

3 cups milk or half and half

1 tsp. salt (to taste)

2 cups cheese (or more if desired)

INSTRUCTIONS

1. Wash hands.
2. Cook macaroni according to package directions.
3. In medium pot, melt butter or margarine. While whisking constantly, pour in flour. Mixture will be very gloppy.
4. Still whisking constantly, slowly pour in milk a little at a time and whisk until lumps are gone.
5. Continue to stir while cooking for about 5 minutes. Mixture will thicken while heating.
6. Add salt and cheese and stir until well blended.
7. Pour mixture over macaroni. Serve immediately.

Substitution tip: Use skim milk to lower the calories and fat.

This is a great take on boxed macaroni and cheese! Homemade and delicious.

MAKE YOUR OWN

/mak/ /yor/ /on/ (*noun*)

to adapt (something) to oneself so that it belongs to oneself.

BETTER THAN THE PACKET TACO SEASONING

Serving size: 1 Tbsp. • Serves: 10.5 (total ⅔ cup)

NUTRITIONAL INFORMATION

Calories: 14 kcals • Carbohydrates: 3 g • Protein: 0.5 g • Fat: 0 g

VEGETARIAN/VEGAN BUDGET SAVER

INGREDIENTS

2-3 Tbsp. dried chopped onions

2 ½ Tbsp. cumin powder

3 Tbsp. chili powder

1 tsp. cornstarch

2 tsp. garlic powder

1 tsp. salt

¼ tsp. cayenne pepper (can add more if you want to dial up the heat)

INSTRUCTIONS

1. Combine all ingredients in an airtight container.

TO USE

2. Cook 1 pound of ground beef until brown
3. Drain beef in colander and rinse with cold water. Pat dry with paper towel.
4. Return to frying pan. Add ¼ cup spice mix and ⅛-¼ cup water (depending on desired consistency).
5. Stir while heating until thoroughly mixed.
6. Use for tacos, enchiladas, or taco salad.

Preparation tip: Double the recipe to make it last longer.

Variation tip: Play around with different amounts of spices to find your favorite combination and flavor style.

Use in Taco Soup (pg 113).

PESTO

Serving size: 2 Tbsp. • Serves: 8

NUTRITIONAL INFORMATION

Calories: 73 kcals • Carbohydrates: 2 g • Protein: 2 g • Fat: 7 g

MAKE AHEAD VEGETARIAN/VEGAN

INGREDIENTS

2 cups fresh basil leaves

2 Tbsp. pine nuts (toasted, if desired)

1 small clove garlic (roasted, if desired)

¼ cup parmesan cheese

½ tsp. salt

2-3 Tbsp. extra virgin olive oil

pepper to taste (optional)

INSTRUCTIONS

1. Wash hands.
2. Combine all ingredients except oil in the blender or food processor for 1 minute, or until smooth.
3. With the motor still running, add oil in a steady stream to combine together.
4. Serve on pasta, with bread, as a sandwich spread, or however desired.

A great way to use up garden basil.

Tip: Use as a spread on sandwiches or on pasta.

Use in Lemon Pesto Chicken with Asparagus and Tomatoes (pg 64) or Chicken Pizza with Pesto Sauce (pg 74).

HOMEMADE SPAGHETTI SAUCE

Serving size: ½ cup • Serves: 6

NUTRITIONAL INFORMATION

Calories: 14 kcals • Carbohydrates: 35 g • Protein: 0.5 g • Fat: 0 g

MAKE AHEAD · QUICK AND EASY · VEGETARIAN/VEGAN · FREEZES WELL

INGREDIENTS

2 oz. tomato sauce

¼ medium onion

¼ tsp. minced garlic

7 oz. diced tomatoes

Italian seasoning (to taste)

salt and pepper (to taste)

extra tomato paste if too thin

extra water if too thick

vegetables (zucchini, spinach, bell peppers) for a more chunkier sauce (optional)

INSTRUCTIONS

1. Wash hands.
2. Blend tomato sauce, onion, and garlic in a blender.
3. Stir in diced tomatoes.
4. Add Italian seasoning, salt, and pepper. Adjust amounts as needed.
5. If needed, add tomato paste or water to adjust thickening to your liking.
6. Use in lasagna, spaghetti, chicken Parmesan, or any other desired dish.

Storage tip: Double the recipe and freeze.

Nutrition tip: Adding extra veggies increases the fiber and nutrients in your sauce.

Recipe courtesy of Kami Quist

HOMEMADE COCOA MIX

Serving size: ¼ cup dry mix • Serves: 40–48

NUTRITIONAL INFORMATION

Calories: 75 kcals • Carbohydrates: 14 g • Protein: 2 g • Fat: 1 g

MAKE AHEAD QUICK AND EASY VEGETARIAN/VEGAN MAKE ONCE EAT TWICE

INGREDIENTS

11 cups instant nonfat dry milk

1¼ cups powdered sugar

1 pound Nestle Nesquik (or similar)

12-oz. jar powdered Coffee Mate (or similar)

INSTRUCTIONS

1. Wash hands.
2. Mix all ingredients together. Store in an airtight container.
3. To make: mix ⅓ cup dry mix with ⅔ cup boiling water.

Variation tip: Add some vanilla or cinnamon for a different flavor hot cocoa.

Pair with Cinnamon and Brown Sugar Almonds (pg 14) for a yummy holiday combination.

MUFFIN MIX (LARGE BATCH)

Serving size: 1 muffin • Serves: 24 per batch (5 large batches)

NUTRITIONAL INFORMATION (per muffin)
Calories: 120 kcals • Carbohydrates: 20 g • Protein: 3 g • Fat: 3 g

MAKE AHEAD QUICK AND EASY BUDGET SAVER MAKE ONCE EAT TWICE FREEZES WELL

INGREDIENTS

17½ cups flour (white, wheat, or a mixture)

2½ cups powdered milk

5 cups sugar

6 Tbsp. + 2 tsp. baking powder

1 Tbsp. + 2 tsp. salt

5 Tbsp. Ener-G egg replacer (found in the health food or gluten-free section of most grocery stores; you can omit this and add a fresh egg and decrease water by 2 Tbsp. when mixing muffins)

Combine all ingredients and store until needed. This amount makes 5 large batches (24 muffins in each batch)

INSTRUCTIONS TO MAKE MUFFINS

INGREDIENTS:

1. 5 cups muffin mix
2. 1¾ cup water
3. ⅓ cup oil
4. ⅓ cup applesauce
5. Any mix-ins you prefer (diced apples and cinnamon, 1 cup frozen or fresh blueberries, 1 cup frozen cranberries chopped slightly in blender, 1 banana mashed or diced, ½ cup raisins)

INSTRUCTIONS TO MAKE WHOLE BATCH

6. Wash hands.
7. Preheat oven to 375.
8. Mix dry/wet ingredients just until blended.
9. Add any mix-ins.
10. Spray muffin tins with spray (don't use paper liners–they will stick).
11. Mound batter into muffin cups.
12. Bake 17–20 minutes.

This make-ahead mix is a great way to get fast muffins, but control what goes into them.

Place all ingredients in a large, airtight container (or 2 gallon Ziploc bag).

Tip: Freeze leftovers for a quick breakfast or snack on the go.

Tip: Add fruit for added vitamins and minerals or nuts for a boost of healthy fats.

This pairs well with Orange Julius (pg 24) and Breakfast Casserole (pg 32).

Recipe courtesy of Patty White

APPENDIX

Non-recipe Meals 198
Measuring Equivalents 201
Common Spices to Use 201
Food Yields 203
Serving Sizes of Common Foods 204
Spice Combination for Ethnic Dishes 205
Preparation Ideas for Fruits 206
Preparation Ideas for Vegetables 207
Ripening of Fruits and Vegetables 208
"Planned" Overs 208
Leftover Cake 210
Food Substitutions 211
Storage Time for Fresh Foods 212
Storage Time for Frozen Foods 213
Beef Cuts 214
Glossary 215

NON-RECIPE MEALS

• BREAKFAST •

YOGURT PARFAITS: Layer in glass any combination of yogurt, granola, and fruit.

SMOOTHIES: Blend any combination of fruit, ice (or use frozen fruit and eliminate ice), fruit juice or milk, yogurt, honey, or sugar. For green smoothies, add spinach or kale. (A quick combo we use is vanilla yogurt, frozen strawberries, milk, and a little sugar. This gives a quick burst of calcium, protein, and vitamins).

EGG SANDWICH: Toast either bread or English muffins. Fry an egg in a skillet. Top with cheese (optional) and insert between slices of toast or English muffins.

FRENCH TOAST: Whip eggs in a bowl with a little milk. Add a dash of salt and some cinnamon (optional). Dip bread into egg mixture and grill on griddle or in a frying pan a few minutes on each side.

EGGS: Omelet, scrambled eggs, boiled eggs, sunny side up, and so on.

OATMEAL: Heat 1 cup water or milk to boiling. Add ½ cup oats with a pinch of salt and stir. Add sweetener to taste. Can also mix in cream, any type of fruit, or granola.

TOAST: (avocado, peanut butter & banana, etc.)—on freshly toasted bread, add slices of avocado, or peanut butter, or peanut butter and sliced bananas. Turns plain toast into a tasty meal.

BREAKFAST BURRITO: Scramble eggs, top with cheese. Optional: Add chopped ham, spinach, or peppers. Spoon onto warmed tortillas and wrap.

• LUNCH/DINNER •

GRILLED CHEESE SANDWICH: Heat griddle or frying pan on medium heat—butter two slices of bread (could put pesto on the inside of one piece for added yum!). Put a slice of cheese in the middle (keep the buttered sides facing out). Cook on griddle or frying pan a few minutes on each side, until golden brown and cheese is melted.

FLAT BREAD PIZZA: Top a piece of flatbread with marinara sauce, cheese, and any toppings you like. Back in oven at 350 for a few minutes, until cheese is melted.

PITA PIZZA: Use pita bread, then follow flat bread pizza directions.

HAWAIIAN HAYSTACKS: Pile on plate any combination of: cooked rice, shredded chicken, gravy (or warmed cream of chicken soup mixed with sour cream instead of milk to make thick), chow mien noodles, frozen peas (thawed), chopped green onions, and cheese.

NON-RECIPE

TACOS/TACO SALAD: Layer on a plate over crushed tortillas (or in a tortilla shell) any combination of: cooked ground beef with taco seasoning, cheese, lettuce, salsa, sour cream, optional: corn, refried beans, black beans, cilantro, ranch)

QUESADILLAS: Top one flour tortilla with any combination of: grilled chicken, beans, cheese, ground or shredded beef. Cover with another tortilla and cook either in microwave or in a skillet on stove.

BAKED POTATO BAR: Bake potatoes in oven at 400 for about 60 min, until very soft. Top with any combination of: cheese, chili, ham, green onions, bacon, chives, butter, salt, pepper.

MASHED POTATOES: Scrub or peel 5–6 potatoes (for portions—use 3 potatoes per person). Chop into medium pieces and place in large pot filled with water. Generously salt water (about 1 Tbsp. for every 6 potatoes) and boil potatoes for about 20 minutes (until a fork can easily slide through a potato piece). Drain water and pour potatoes into mixing bowl. For flavoring, add any mixture of milk (about ¼ cup), butter, salt, sour cream, cream cheese, garlic powder (optional), chicken bouillon (optional). Mix with mixer until smooth and creamy. Serve alone or with gravy.

GRAVY:

Option 1: when cooking meat, pour meat drippings into medium pot. In separate bowl, mix ¼ cup flour with about 1 cup cold water and stir to remove lumps. While stirring the meat drippings, slowly pour in flour slurry and continue to stir until thickened. Can add more water if needed.

Option 2: when not cooking meat, heat 1 cup chicken broth (or 1 cup water with 2 cubes bouillon) to boiling. Follow same flour slurry directions as option 1. Stir flour slurry into chicken broth and stiff with a whisk until thickened. Can add salt/pepper to taste.

ROUX:

Use equal amounts of butter and flour, then add milk (or cream or half and half) and salt

For example: melt ½ cup butter in sauce pan. Whisk in ½ cup flour (with 1 tsp. salt added in). It will become clumpy. Keep whisking and stir in 3 cups milk (or cream, or half and half). Continue stirring constantly until smooth and thickened. (Can add more milk if you want it less thick.)

Option 1 (white sauce): Add it to soups to make it a creamy soup, or serve over potatoes or with peas, hamburger or ham.

Option 2 (cheese sauce): Add cheese (1–2 cups) to turn the roux into a cheesy sauce (great over potatoes, broccoli, cauliflower, or noodles to make a homemade mac and cheese!), or can add to soups to make it a cheesy soup.

SPAGHETTI: Boil spaghetti noodles of choice 7–10 minutes, until soft (can squish with a fork to make sure it's cooked through). Drain water. Top with spaghetti sauce (optional—can heat spaghetti sauce with cooked ground beef or cooked meatballs) (optional—top with Parmesan cheese)

MEATBALL SUBS: heat frozen meatballs with spaghetti sauce. Spoon saucy meatballs into sub sandwich rolls (only cut one side, so the back is still together to capture all of the sauce. Top with provolone cheese slice, squish together, and enjoy! (Keep a napkin handy—it gets messy.)

STROMBOLI: Unroll refrigerated tube container of Pillsbury (or generic) French bread dough. On a greased cookie sheet. Cut slits down each side, leaving thick strip down center intact. Top center strip with either 1. Chopped ham and cheese or 2. Pizza toppings (pizza sauce, cheese, possibly pepperoni or ham). With the side slits, make an X over the center, criss crossing each side, working down the entire length. Bake at 350 for 25 min, until top is golden brown. Take out and rub butter over the top. Slice and serve.

FAJITAS: Grill any combination of steak (or chicken) pieces, sliced onions, sliced peppers. Fill tortilla and top with sour cream, guacamole, and salsa.

CHILI: Any type of beans (black, kidney, red, chili), add ground beef, a couple stalks of chopped celery, 1 big can of stewed tomatoes (or diced, or any type of canned tomato), salt (about 1 tsp), pinch of pepper, 1–2 tsp. of chili powder, cayenne pepper (if you want it spicy), optional: cumin. Pour all together either in a slow cooker and let simmer all day, or in a regular pot and heat over a stove, cooking occasionally until heated through.

SALAD IN A JAR: Mix any type of lettuce, spinach, kale, shredded or sliced carrots, sliced cucumber, celery, or any other vegetable you have on hand. Place in a jar. When ready to eat, pour in some salad dressing and shake. Can eat straight from the jar.

NACHOS: Spread tortilla chips on a plate, cover with shredded cheese. Heat in microwave until cheese is melted.

HAMBURGERS: Mix fresh ground beef with 1 egg, salt, pepper, a little Worcestershire sauce, and barbecue sauce. Form into patties and cook on a grill, griddle, or in a frying pan until cooked through.

SANDWICHES (BLT, TUNA, ETC.): Can add any combination of sandwich meats, lettuce, tomatoes, cucumbers (picture walking down a the sandwich lane at subway—almost anything goes on a sandwich!). For Tuna sandwiches, look for tuna packed in water. Open can and drain water. Mix with a couple spoonfuls of mayonnaise. Can also Add chopped pickles or celery. Spread on bread. Can also toast the bread for toasted tuna sandwiches. For a great twist on a classic Peanut butter and Jelly sandwich, 1. Add sliced bananas, or 2. Turn it into a grilled PB&J sandwich. Make as usual, but spread butter on the outer sides and grill until golden brown.

CHEF SALAD: Add chopped ham or turkey to any regular salad. Can also add cheese, chopped up boiled eggs, and bacon.

WRAPS: Like sandwiches, anything goes with wraps. From meat to cheese, to peanut butter and jelly, simply place on tortilla and wrap up. For a lower calorie option, you can omit the tortilla and use lettuce as the wrap.

PASTA SALAD: cooked pasta (bow tie, elbow macaroni, etc.), mixed veggies, ranch dressing packet.

CAPRESE: Slice tomatoes and spread on a plate. Top each tomato slice with fresh, sliced mozzarella cheese. Top with basil leave and lightly shake balsamic vinegar, olive oil, and salt.

MEASURING EQUIVALENTS

3 teaspoons = 1 tablespoon
5 1/3 tablespoons = 1/3 cup
12 tablespoons = 3/4 cup
16 ounces = 1 pound
1 cup = 8 fluid ounces
2 cups = 1 pint
4 quarts = 1 gallon
4 tablespoons = 1/4 cup
8 tablespoons = ½ cup
16 tablespoons = 1 cup
2 tablespoons = 1 fluid ounce
1 cup = ½ pint
4 cups = 1 quart

• ABBREVIATIONS •

Tbsp. = tablespoon tsp. = teaspoon oz. = ounces

COMMON SPICES

ALLSPICE: Tastes like a combination of cloves, cinnamon, and nutmeg. Whole allspice is good for seasoning pot roast, stews, and ham. Ground allspice is good for mincemeat and pumpkin pie, plum pudding, cookies, cakes, and some vegetables (squash, turnips, carrots).

BASIL: An important seasoning in tomato dishes. Also good in soups, stews, and as a seasoning for beans, peas, and squash. Sprinkle on lamb before cooking.

BAY LEAVES: Use in soups and stews. They make an excellent addition to fish chowder. Use in a variety of meat dishes such as beef and lamb.

CARAWAY: Gives rye bread its distinctive flavor. A frequent addition to rolls, cakes, and cheeses. Also good in cottage cheese. Add to turnips and asparagus when cooking.

CELERY SEED: Use in sauces, salads, salad dressings, fish, meat, and vegetables. Sprinkle over cheese, crackers, or rolls.

CHILI POWDER: Good in seafood cocktail sauces and barbecue sauces. Try it in meatloaf, hamburger, stews, and chili.

CHIVES: Recommended in salads and salad dressings, scrambled eggs, omelets. Add to cream cheese and cottage cheese.

CINNAMON: Good in combination with apples in baked dishes and pies. Can be used in a variety of baked goods. Sprinkle over puddings and hot cereal. Combine with mashed sweet potatoes. Use in French toast.

CLOVES: Whole cloves are good in roast pork, ham, pickled fruits, spicy syrup, and meat gravies. Ground cloves are good in baked goods, chocolate pudding, stews, and vegetables.

CORIANDER: Can be used in Spanish rice and in curry blends.

CUMIN: WHOLE: Chili con carne, hot tamales, soups, cheese, meat, and rice dishes Ground: Deviled eggs, meat loaf, croquettes, cheese spreads

CURRY POWDER: Use in curry sauces for curried eggs, vegetables, fish, and meat. Try a dash in French dressing, scalloped tomatoes, clam and fish chowders, and split pea soup

DILL SEED: Adds a bright touch to rye and pumpernickel bread, soups, salads, sauces, meat and fish dishes, potatoes and coleslaw

FENNEL: Comes both whole and ground. Used extensively for breads, rolls, and pastries. Also used in seasoning for soups, fruit dishes, and sauces.

GARLIC: soups, salads, meats, fish, pasta, and casserole dishes. Refried and plain black beans. Salsa, mashed potatoes.

GINGER: Use in cookies, spice cakes, ginger bread. Also good in pot roast, stews, chicken, soups, and fish dishes.

MARJORAM: Excellent seasoning for vegetables (green beans, lima beans, and peas). Enhances the flavor of lamb, stews, and poultry.

NUTMEG: Use in flavoring baked goods, rice and custard pudding, vegetables, and in beverages. Add to vegetables and soups, beef and fish dishes.

OREGANO: An essential ingredient in chili powder. A classic addition to almost any tomato dish, vegetable or salad.

PAPRIKA: Use as a garnish for colorless foods. It brightens fish, and salads.

BLACK PEPPER: Ground and cracked: In meats, sauces, gravies, many vegetables, soup, salads, and eggs.

CAYENNE PEPPER: Used in deviled ham and eggs, cheese canapés, barbecue sauces, and stews.

RED PEPPER: Whole: Pickles, relishes, hot sauces.
Crushed: Sauces, pickles, highly spiced meats
Ground: Meats, sauces, fish, and egg dishes

POULTRY SEASONING: For poultry, veal, pork, and fish stuffing. Good with paprika for meat loaf.

ROSEMARY: Available ground or whole. Wonderful with boiled potatoes, turnips, and cauliflower. Sprinkle on beef, chicken, and fish before cooking.

SAFFRON: Adds a distinctive flavor to rolls and cakes. Particularly good with rice.

SAGE WHOLE AND GROUND: Perfect accompaniment for pork and poultry.

THYME: Great in savory dishes, like braised meat, vegetables, or fish.

FOOD YIELDS

APPLES 1 pound = 3 medium = 3 cups sliced

BANANAS 1 pound = 3–4 medium = 11/3 cups mashed = 2 1/2 cups sliced

BEANS (dry) 1 pound = 2 1/2 cups (dry) = 5 1/2 cups cooked

BREAD 1 pound loaf = 16 slices

BREAD CRUMBS 8 ounces = 2 1/4 cups crumbs

3–4 SLICES BREAD = 1 cup bread crumbs

BUTTER, MARGARINE, SHORTENING 1 pound = 2 cups

CABBAGE 1 pound = 4 cups shredded

CARROTS 1 pound = 3 cups sliced, raw; 6 regular carrots = 1 pound, 48 baby carrots = 1 pound; 12 baby carrots = 1 cup shredded; 2 medium carrots

EGGS (medium) 1 dozen = 2 cups

EGG WHITES 1 dozen = 1 1/3 cups

FLOUR, ALL-PURPOSE 1 pound = 4 cups sifted

FLOUR, WHOLE WHEAT 1 pound = 3 1/2 ups

GRAHAM CRACKERS 15 crackers = 1 cup crumbs

GROUND MEAT (beef, pork, turkey) 1 pound = 2 cups cooked

HONEY 1 pound = 1 1/3 cups

LEMONS 1 medium lemon = 3–4 tablespoons juice

MACARONI, SPAGHETTI 1 pound = 3 3/4 cups dry = 9 cups cooked

MILK, EVAPORATED 6 ounce can = 1 1/2 cups diluted

NOODLES 1 pound = 6 cups (dry) = 8 cups cooked

OATMEAL 1 pound dry = 5 cups (dry) = 2.5 cups cooked

ONIONS 1 pound = 3 large; 1 cup = 1.5–2 medium onions

POTATOES 1 pound = 3 medium = 3 cups sliced = 1 3/4 cup mashed; 1 cup chopped = 1.5 medium

RAISINS 1 pound = 3 cups

RICE, REGULAR WHITE 1 pound = 2 1/4 cups (dry) = 8 cups cooked

SALTINES 25 crackers = 1 cup crumbs

SUGAR, WHITE GRANULATED 1 pound = 2 cups

SUGAR, BROWN 1 pound = 2 1/4 cup (firmly packed)

YEAST (ACTIVE DRY) 1 packet = 1 tablespoon

SERVING SIZES OF COMMON FOODS

FRUIT

1 medium whole fruit (½ banana) (about the size of a tennis ball)
½ cup fresh fruit cut up
¼ cup dried fruit
½ cup fruit juice

VEGETABLE

1 cup fresh leafy green
½ cup cut up fresh vegetables
1 medium potato (about the size of a computer mouse)
½ cup cooked vegetables
½ cup vegetable juice

MEAT

3 ounces cooked meat (the size of a deck of cards)
1 egg
2 egg whites

GRAINS

1 slice bread
1 small tortilla
1 small pancake (about the size of a DVD)
1 cup cereal
½ cup cooked pasta
½ cup rice (about the size of a baseball)
1 cup popcorn (air popped)

DAIRY

1 cup milk
1 cup yogurt
1.5 oz. cheese (about the size of 2 dice)

NUTS/SEEDS

2 Tbsp. Peanut Butter (about the size of a golf ball)
2 Tbsp. Nuts (fits in the palm of your hand)

FATS/OILS

1 Tbsp. margarine, butter, oil

SPICE COMBINATION FOR ETHNIC DISHES

Most ethnic dishes use varieties of the same grouping of spices. Having the group of spices on hand will help you make the majority of dishes in that particular cuisine.

BASIC

Salt
Pepper
Italian blend
Cumin
Garlic powder
Onion powder
Cinnamon
Ginger

MEDITERRANEAN

Cumin
Cinnamon
Garlic powder
Basil
Bay leaf
Paprika
Fennel
Dill
Sage
Savory
Marjoram
Turmeric
Oregano
Parsley

ITALIAN

Italian blend
Basil
Oregano
Garlic Powder
Parsley
Sage
Rosemary

GREEK

Oregano
Garlic powder
Onion
Dill
Marjoram
Thyme
Parsley
Rosemary
Cinnamon

INDIAN

Curry
Turmeric
Coriander
Cumin
Mustard powder
Clove
Cardamom
Masala
Ginger
Fenugreek

MEXICAN

Cumin
Chili powder
Oregano
Onion powder
Garlic
Cilantro

PREPARATION IDEAS FOR FRUITS

APPLE: applesauce, baked, fresh wedges, juice, pudding, tapioca, raisin salad, prepare the "guts" to an apple pie

APRICOT: in fruit cups, plain, stewed, whipped, dried

BANANA: baked (in bread and muffins), in fruit cups, in gelatin, in orange juice, pudding, sliced, whole or half, with milk, frozen, smoothie, dipped in chocolate

BERRIES: plain, with milk or cream (fresh or frozen)

CANTALOUPE: balls, in fruit cups, sliced or cubed

CHERRIES (PITTED): plain, in gelatin, in pudding, frozen, cherry cobbler, pie

GRAPEFRUIT: juice, salad, sections

GRAPES (SEEDLESS): in gelatin, plain, in fruit salad, in lettuce salad, in chicken salad sandwiches, frozen

MELONS: balls, cubes, in fruit cups, sliced

ORANGES: in custard, juice, sections, wedges, freeze peeled slices, in smoothie

PEACHES: in gelatin, plain, sliced, halved, salad, sauce, dried, tapioca, fruit cobbler, fresh pie

PEARS: plain, with cheese, sauce, in salads, stewed, dried, sauce

PINEAPPLE: crushed, cubed, plain, with sweet and sour chicken, juice, in smoothies

PLUMS: plain, in juice, dried, stewed

PUMPKIN: baked, custard, mashed, cooked whole (cut lid, remove seeds, and roast), in muffins, bread, pancakes

PREPARATION IDEAS FOR VEGETABLES

BEANS (LIMA): raw, cooked with bacon or ham, with tomatoes

BEANS (SNAP): raw, with crisp bacon chips, with cream sauce, with tomatoes, with carrot circles, in salad, steamed

BEETS: buttered, cold sliced, lettuce, salad

BROCCOLI: raw, buttered, with lemon sauce, with cheese sauce, with cream sauce, in casseroles, steamed, in soups

CABBAGE: cooked with carrots, coleslaw, creamed, raw wedge, salad, sauerkraut

CARROTS: raw sticks, curls, wheels, baked, cooked with celery, cooked with peas, creamed, glazed, raisin salad, cake or cupcakes, in soups or stews, mashed, cabbage slaw

CAULIFLOWER: raw, with cheese sauce, steamed, with cream sauce, with peas

CELERY: raw sticks, with peanut butter, braised, cooked with carrots, in chili or stews

CORN: on the cob, steamed, with lima beans, popped, homemade pizza, in chili, in cooked salsa

CUCUMBER: raw slices, in salads

GREEN PEAS (SNOW): raw, sautéed, steamed, in stir fry

GREENS: steamed, creamed, raw leaf, with celery, with hard-cooked eggs, with cheese sauce

LETTUCE: raw, shredded, combination salad, wedges, chicken wraps

PARSNIPS: browned, raw strips

POTATOES: baked, boiled, with cheese sauce, mashed, hash browns, in soups or stews, scalloped

RUTABAGAS: cubed, mashed, raw strips

SQUASH (SUMMER): raw sticks, curls, wheels, steamed, with tomato, seasoned with bacon or onion and baked

SQUASH (WINTER): baked, mashed, cooked in shell, roast seeds

SWEET POTATO: baked, mashed, scalloped with apple, boiled

TOMATO: raw edges or slices, baked, broiled, juiced, scalloped, stewed, salsa, bruschetta, salads, on sandwiches

RIPENING OF FRUITS AND VEGETABLES

FRUITS THAT RIPEN AFTER BEING PICKED
Apricots, Avocados, Bananas, Cantaloupe, Honeydew, Kiwifruits, Nectarines, Papaya, Peaches, Pears, Plantains, Plums, Tomatoes

FOODS THAT DON'T RIPEN AFTER PICKING
Apples, Berries, Cherries, Grapefruit, Grapes, Lemons, Limes, Oranges, Pineapple, Strawberries, Tangerines, Watermelon

"PLANNED" OVERS

Turn leftovers into "planned" overs by knowing ahead of time how you can use extra food from one meal to make a whole new dish.

RICE

- Sauté with onion. Then simmer in bouillon or broth with soy sauce to taste. Add thin strips of leftover meat to make a complete meal.
- Make into rice pudding.
- Turn into cheesy rice. Sprinkle cheese on top and heat until cheese is melted. Stir to mix all together.

EGGS

- Add whites for meringues.
- Add whites or yolks to scrambled eggs in the morning.

BREAD

- Butter, cube, and toast for croutons to garnish soups and salads.
- Crush with rolling pin and store in sealed container for crumbs in breading meats or making stuffing.

CAKE

- Break into pieces and mix with fruit and pudding. Refrigerate and serve for dessert with whipped topping.

FRUIT

- Combine with yogurt.
- Add to salads.
- Make Jell-O salad.
- Freeze to use in smoothies.

VEGETABLES

- Add to soups or casseroles.
- Marinate, chill, and serve in salads.
- Make a quick pasta salad.
- Freeze for use in future soups or casseroles.
- Put into spaghetti or lasagna dishes.
- Add to chili.

CHICKEN

- Chop or shred extra and use in chicken quesadillas, tacos, meatloaf, or any type of chicken casserole.

ROAST

- Layer extra with veggies and leftover gravy. Top with leftover mashed potatoes for a roast version of shepherd's pie. Freeze in a Ziploc bag and add to stews or soups.
-

GROUND MEAT

- Use in a pot of chili, mix with taco seasoning for tacos or taco salad, or use in sloppy joes.

MASHED POTATOES

- Shape into round patties and chill or freeze between sheets of waxed paper. To cook, brown in greased skillet and season to taste.

BAKED POTATOES

- Shred for hash browns.
- Chop for use in potato salad.
- Dice and fry in skillet to make fried spuds.
- Shred and combine with cream of chicken soup, sour cream, cheese, and sautéed onions and butter to make cheesy potatoes.

WAFFLES OR PANCAKES

- Chill or freeze in layers between waxed paper. Reheat in a single layer at 400 degrees turning once.
- Serve with creamed chicken for a main course or with ice cream and fruit for dessert.

LEFTOVER CAKE

When you've exhausted all efforts to use up the leftovers, there's only one thing left to do. Let them eat cake! Two variations—a chocolate and a spice cake—make using your leftovers fun and sweet.

INGREDIENTS

1½ cups flour

1½ cup sugar

2 tsp. baking powder

1 tsp. baking soda

½ tsp. salt

½ cup cocoa powder for chocolate (OR 1 Tbsp. pumpkin pie spice for spice cake)

½ cup vegetable oil

2 eggs

1 tsp. vanilla

enough leftovers to make 2 cups puree, the consistency of baby food (Anything goes here–the chocolate or spice of the cake covers it up. If it is too thick, add water or applesauce.)

INSTRUCTIONS

1. Wash hands.
2. Preheat oven to 350 degrees.
3. Mix dry ingredients in a bowl.
4. Add wet ingredients until combined.
5. Spray 9x12 pan or 12 cupcake tins with cooking spray and pour in batter.
6. Bake 35 minutes (20 min. for cupcakes).
7. Serve topped with frosting, ice cream, canned pie filling, sifted powdered sugar, or plain.
8. Cake freezes wonderfully.

TIP: If you don't have pumpkin pie spice for the spice cake, substitute: 1¼ tsp. cinnamon, ½ tsp. nutmeg, and ¼ tsp. cloves.

• CHOCOLATE OR SPICE CAKE •

FOOD SUBSTITUTIONS

Out of an ingredient? No problem. Before heading to the store, check out these quick substitutions you can make with items you already have on hand.

INGREDIENT	AMOUNT	SUBSTITUTIONS
Baking Powder	1 teaspoon	¼ tsp. baking soda plus 5/8 tsp cream of tartar, or ¼ tsp baking soda plus ½ cup sour milk or butter milk (decrease liquid called for in recipe by ½ cup).
Beef of Chicken Broth	1 cup	2 tsp. instant beef or chicken bouillon granules or 1-2 cubes) added to 1 cup boiling water.
Bouillon Cube	1	1 Tbsp. soy sauce.
Dry bread crumbs	¼ cup	¼ cup cracker crumbs, corn meal, or cut up fresh bread (1 piece) and bake in oven, turning every few minutes, until dry, then place in zip lock bag and crumble.
Butter	1 cup	1 cup shortening plus ½ tsp. salt or 1 cup margarine.
Catsup or chili sauce	1 cup	1 cup tomato sauce plus ½ cup sugar and 1 tbsp. vinegar (to use in cooking only).
Chicken	1 whole	8 thighs, or 3 breasts, or 8 legs, or 4 legs and thighs.
Corn Syrup	1 cup	1 cup sugar plus ¼ cup liquid (use whatever liquid is called for in recipe)
Cornstarch (as thickener)	1 Tbsp.	2 tbsp. all-purpose flour, or 2 tbsp quick cooking tapioca
Egg (in cake batter only)	1	2 tbsp mayonnaise
Flour, all purpose	1 cup sifted	1 cup plus 2 tbsp. sifted cake flour or 1 cup unsifted all-purpose flour minus 2 tbsp.
Flour, all purpose	1 tbsp	(for thickening) ½ tbsp. cornstarch or quick cooking tapioca.
Garlic	1 clove small	1/8 tsp. garlic powder.
Gelatin, Flavored	3 oz. package	1 tbsp plain gelatin plus 2 cups fruit juice.
Herbs, fresh	1 tbsp.	1 tsp dried herbs
Honey	1 cup	1 ½ cups sugar plus ¼ cup liquid (use what's called for in the recipe)
Lemon 1 medium	1 tsp	2-3 tbsp. juice and 1-2 tsp rind ½ tsp vinegar
Milk, Buttermilk	1 cup	1 cup yogurt, or 1 tbsp. vinegar or lemon juice plus milk to equal 1 cup

Milk, Whole	1 cup	½ cup evaporated milk plus ½ cup water
Milk, skim	1 cup	5 tbsp nonfat dry milk and 1 cup water
Onion, fresh	1 small	1 tbsp minced onion rehydrated
Prepared Mustard	1 tbsp	1 tsp. dried mustard
Parsley, dried	1 tsp.	3 tsp chopped fresh parsley
Sour Cream	1 cup	1 cup yogurt
Sugar, White	1 cup	1 cup corn syrup minus ¼ cup liquid in recipe or 1 cup powdered sugar, or 1 cup brown sugar or 1 cup honey (reduce liquid in recipe by ¼ cup)
Tomato Juice	1 cup	½ tomato sauce plus ¼ cup water
Tomato Sauce	1 can (15 oz)	1 can tomato paste and 1 can water
Tomatoes	1 can	3 fresh medium tomatoes, cut up
Yogurt	1 cup	1 cup buttermilk or sour milk (1 tbsp vinegar or lemon juice plus milk equal to 1 cup) let stand 5 minutes until thickened.

STORAGE TIME FOR FRESH FOODS

FOR BEST RESULTS, USE WITHIN THE SPECIFIED TIME FRAME.

FRESH FRUITS	DAYS	WEEKS	MONTHS
Apples			1
Apricots, Bananas, Grapes, Nectarines, Peaches, Pears, Plums, Watermelon	3–5		
Berries, Cherries	2–3		
Cranberries, Melons (except watermelon)		1	

FRESH VEGETABLES	DAYS	WEEKS	MONTHS
Beans (snap or wax), Cauliflower, Celery, Cucumber, Eggplant, Green Peppers, Salad Greens, Turnips		2	
Beets, Carrots, Parsnips, Radishes, Rutabagas, Turnips		2	
Broccoli, Brussels Sprouts, Greens (Spinach, Kale, Collards. Etc), Okra, Onions (Green), Peas, Summer Squash	3–5		
Cabbage		1–2	
Corn	Asap		

MEATS	DAYS	WEEKS	MONTHS
Roasts, Steaks, Chips	3–5		
Ground Meat, Stew Meat, Poultry, Fish,, Variety Meats	1–2		
Cured and Smoked Meats (Frankfurters, Bacon, Sausage, Whole Ham)			1
Cooked Meats and Meat Dishes	3–4		
Gravy and Broth	1–2		

DAIRY	DAYS	WEEKS	MONTHS
Milk		1	
Cottage Cheese	5–7		
Hard Cheeses		Several	
Eggs Raw, Hardboiled, in shell, Hardboiled, peeled	5		

STORAGE TIME FOR FROZEN FOOD

FOR BEST RESULTS, USE WITHIN THE SPECIFIED NUMBER OF MONTHS.

FRESH FRUITS	MONTHS
Fruits and Fruit Juice Concentrates	12
Vegetables	8
Bread and Yeast Rolls	3

MEAT	MONTHS
Ground Beef	3–4
Beef Roasts and Steaks	6–12
Lamb Roasts	6–9
Cured Pork	1–2
Pork Roasts	4–8
Cooked Meat Dishes	2–3

POULTRY	MONTHS
Chicken Parts	9
Turkey Parts	6
Chicken or Turkey, Whole	12
Cooked Chicken or Turkey	4–6

FISH	MONTHS
Fish Fillets	2–3
Cooked Fish	3

DAIRY	MONTHS
Ice Cream or Sherbet	1
Cheese	Don't freeze
Butter	Several
Milk	Don't freeze

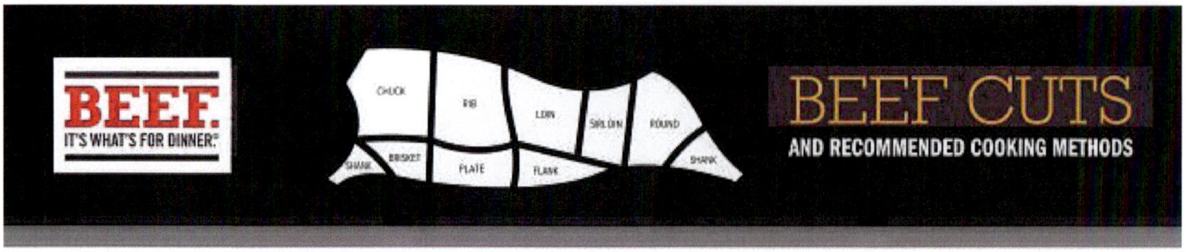

(used with permission from the Beef Council)

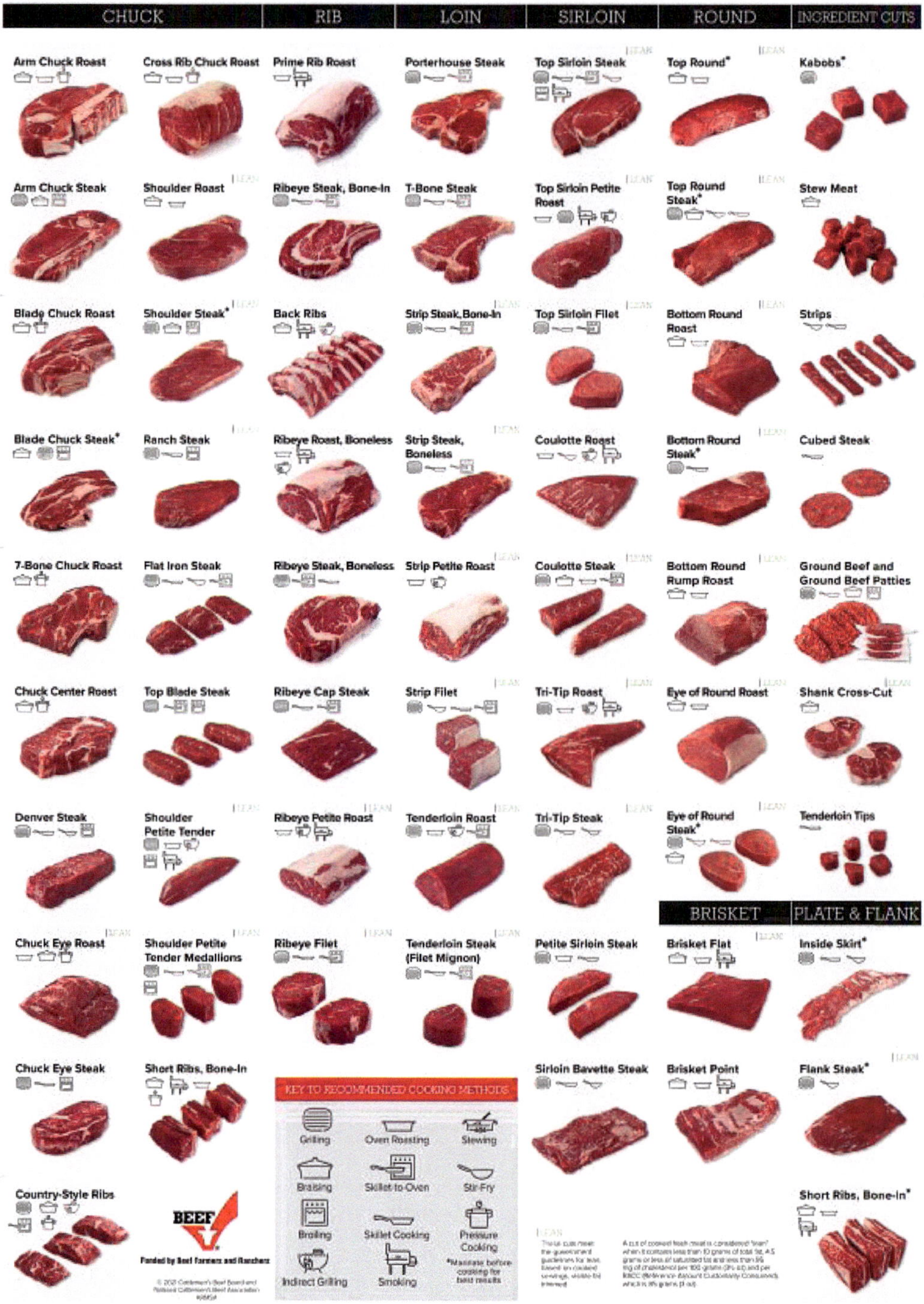